CHRISTOPHER TABRAHAM

SCOTTISH · CASTLES AND FORTIFICATIONS

AN INTRODUCTION TO THE HISTORIC CASTLES, HOUSES AND
ARTILLERY FORTIFICATIONS IN THE CARE OF
THE SECRETARY OF STATE FOR SCOTLAND

Let us explore the ruin'd Abbeys Choir;
It's fretted roof and windows of rich Tracery,
The Sculptur'd Tombs O'ergrown with shrubs and brambles,
'Midst broken arches, graves and gloomy vaults,
Or view the Castle of Some Ancient Thane,
It's Hall, its Dungeons and Embattled Towers
Mantled with Ivy, –

Francis Grose, *Antiquities of Scotland* (1789)

HISTORIC BUILDINGS AND MONUMENTS

Scottish Development Department

EDINBURGH

HER MAJESTY'S STATIONERY OFFICE

Contents

Designed by J Cairns HMSO/GD

Edited by David J Breeze

HER MAJESTY'S STATIONERY OFFICE

Government Bookshops

13a Castle Street, Edinburgh EH2 3AR
49 High Holborn, London WC1V 6HB
Princess Street, Manchester M60 8AS
Southey House, Wine Street, Bristol BS1 2BQ
258 Broad Street, Birmingham B1 2HE
80 Chichester Street, Belfast BT1 4JY

Government publications are also available through booksellers

Crown Copyright 1986
First published 1986
ISBN 0 11 492475 9

CASTLES IN CARE

*"Indeed, all the gentlemen's houses are strong castles, they
being so treacherous one to another, that they are forced to
defend themselves in strongholds."*
(Thomas Kirke, 1679)

MAN'S SEEMING inability to live in peace with his fellow has for long caused him to erect defences to protect both himself and those in his charge. The Scottish landscape is covered with the signs of such endeavours, from prehistoric hill-forts traceable high up in her hills to the defences erected around her coast during World War Two. The most conspicuous defence by far is the medieval castle. Following its appearance in Scotland in the twelfth century AD, it remained a dominant feature of Scottish society until the seventeenth century, by which time firm central government had largely obviated the need for fortress-residences. Thereafter, certain major political disturbances – most notably the revolution and

opposite
Hermitage Castle, "the strength of Liddesdale", built by an Englishman, captured and rebuilt by a Scotsman, and a testimony to the troubled centuries of conflict on Scotland's Border throughout the medieval age.

Kilchurn Castle on Loch Awe – a place of strength until the eighteenth century and one of Scotland's most romantic castles. It was opened to the public in 1984.

Cromwellian interlude of the 1640s and 1650s, and the Jacobite uprisings later that century and into the next – caused government and adversary alike to re-equip certain strategically placed castles in addition to erecting new artillery fortifications.

Scotland is a country as rich in castles and fortifications as any in Europe. From Hermitage Castle, close beside her border with England, to Muness Castle, the northernmost castle in Great Britain, there has survived a remarkable and distinctive series of castellated and domestic buildings from the mightiest of fortresses to the more modest lairds' houses; from the simple earthwork and timber castles introduced by the Anglo-Norman lords in the twelfth century to complex artillery fortifications like Fort George, erected by the Hanoverian government shortly after the 1745–46 Jacobite uprising.

A considerable and largely representative number are now held in trust for the nation by the Secretary of State for Scotland and cared for on his behalf by Historic Buildings and Monuments, Scottish Development Department. A handful have always been in the care of the state, having been constructed for the Crown and financed from the public purse. Indeed, two – Edinburgh Castle and Fort George – still function as military establishments. The majority, however, were

The Queen's Own Highlanders parade on the Esplanade at Edinburgh Castle. A permanent garrison of soldiery has been quartered in the castle since the time of King Charles II.

built for private use, by land-holders great and small, lords and lairds alike. As society evolved and attitudes changed, so these antiquated structures were remodelled, sometimes replaced and ultimately abandoned in favour of more comfortable and amenable residences, which are, in the main, still inhabited and not to be found in the care of the state. The sole exception is Duff House, commissioned from William Adam by William Duff (later Earl Fife) in 1730 and among the finest works of Georgian baroque architecture in the British Isles.

The introduction of Ancient Monuments legislation in 1882 for the first time enabled owners of the best and most representative of these redundant structures to entrust them into the guardianship of the state. A modest twelfth-century earthwork and timber castle deep in Galloway, Druchtag Motehill, led the way, in 1888. Twenty years on, Scalloway Castle, at the opposite end of the country and built in 1600 by the despotic and unscrupulous Patrick Stewart, Earl of Orkney, became the first masonry castle taken into care. They have since been joined by a further three score and more, including an early nineteenth-century Martello tower at Hackness, on Scapa Flow in Orkney.

Each monument is unique, having historical associations and an architectural development all its own. And yet, notwithstanding this individuality, each has to be seen as part of a general development, a response, be it by monarch, nobleman or government, to a particular defensive need at a given time. Many of the monuments are directly linked through family ties, not altogether surprising in a country as small as Scotland where much of the wealth was concentrated in a relatively few hands. Many monuments have a guide-book or leaflet giving the visitor a detailed insight into a particular monument's history and architecture. This book is by way of an introduction to all those castles, houses and artillery fortifications in the care of the Secretary of State for Scotland.

Druchtag Motehill, among the earliest castles built in Scotland and the first to be taken into state care, in 1888. This sketch, from the original papers at the time of transfer, was drawn by Lieutenant-General Augustus Henry Lane-Fox Pitt-Rivers, appointed Her Majesty's first Inspector of Ancient Monuments in 1883.

Castles in care – a stonemason at work on the ageing fabric of Dunstaffnage Castle.

remierement sist larcenesse
de Reins. ¶Apres seoit
lempereur. ¶Apres seoit
le Roy dalemaigne ou mileu
du front de la sale ¶Apres
le Roy de france seoit le roy

des romains. Et anoit autant de distance
du Roy au Roy des romains come du
Roy a lempereur. Et anoient lempriem
le Roy et le Roy des romains chascun se
parement vn ciel de drap dor borde dasur
au aus armes de france. Et par dessus ceuls

THE CASTLE AS RESIDENCE

*"My hallis, gallareis, chalmeris, vardrope, kitchingis,
stabillis, sellaris, lednaris, pantreis, librellis, or wther office
houssis quhatsumewer."*
(Inventory of William Forbes,
7th laird of Tolquhon, 1589)

THE FORM and appearance of the medieval castle was dictated as much by the demands of feudal power and ritual as by any defensive consideration. Feudal society was dominated by pomp and ceremony, power and wealth and those at the top of that society wielding that power built castles that were, outwardly, undeniable statements of their rank and position and, internally, well capable of satisfying all the requirements demanded of them. It was a society so different from our own that our appreciation of the legacy of castle ruins that has come down to us will not be so rewarding if we do not bear this change in mind.

Simply stated, medieval society was more openly structured, less private and familial. The ties of blood were certainly of great importance, but the relationship between lord and vassal greatly enlarged the "family". Those who held land accepted not only the power and wealth that ensued therefrom but also the obligations attached thereto. They were the instruments of local government and administration at all times, and in war were required to contribute their allotted provision towards the Scottish army, or "host". Their castles served not merely as secure houses in a perilous world but were expected to function as administrative centre, barracks, court and hotel as well. To meet these diverse demands, land-holders had little recourse other than to maintain substantial households – office-bearers, retainers, servants and others – whose various duties enabled the exacting demands of administration, hospitality and courtly ritual to be met. No land-holder was exempt, for each in his own way was under obligations. The difference was merely one of degree; the substantial size of household

maintained by the monarch or mighty baron was neither possible nor indeed necessary for the more modestly endowed knight.

The medieval castle was the visible expression of the pride and pomp of the ruling class. Within its walls folk from all ranks of life gathered round their lord, "tied by service and hereditary loyalty, bound together by shared ceremony and ritual, and prepared if needs be to fight for him". Only as feudalism began to wane in the later Middle Ages and the more modern conceptions of comfort, etiquette and sophistication in private life take root did the medieval castle gradually evolve into the country house. Freed from all considerations regarding defence and substantially relieved of the onerous obligations of courtly ceremony, those who built new houses from the reign of James VI on did so with comfort and privacy for the first time their foremost consideration.

The standing and position of a feudal lord was reflected in the complexity of his castle; the higher his station, the larger his household and the greater his provision of halls, chambers, lodgings and service accommodation. Considerable ingenuity was exercised by castle builders throughout the Middle Ages in the disposition of the various elements and each of our castles is unique in this respect. Notwithstanding their individuality of plan, they all share in common the components that combined to make a medieval castle.

At the heart of the castle was the **hall**. Within it many of the legal and administrative obligations of the feudal superior were carried out and here the tenantry assembled when occasion demanded. It

Bronze ewer (fifteenth century) from Urquhart Castle, used to hold water for washing before the meal. (*Royal Museum of Scotland*)

opposite
The two prime functions of a castle, as fortress and as residence, feature on this illumination from the *Grandes Chroniques de France*, by Jean Fouquet. Note the elaborate cloth of estate behind the dais table enhancing the status of the host, in this case King Charles V of France.

The outer or great hall at Doune Castle. The open-timber roof and minstrels' gallery (at the far end) are Victorian restorations, as is the central fire-basket, but that this place has been a splendid chamber, in its day the scene of "large tabling and belly cheer", is immediately obvious to the visitor.

The hall of Earl Patrick Stewart's palace at Kirkwall, arguably the noblest state room of any private castle in Scotland.

The fine stone buffet gracing the fifteenth-century hall at Dirleton Castle, within which the best plate was placed during banquets.

served also as the main living-room for the lord's family and household, where many of them dined and some of them slept, either on shake-downs on the floor or in tiny closets adjacent. The hall was the place for "large tabling and belly cheer" and, relatively poor though the country was, the reputation of Scots for being generous, some would say overgenerous, hosts is of long standing. A visitor to Scotland in James VI's reign was struck by the fact that "the Scots of the better sort spend the great part of the night in drinking", and another, Thomas Kirke, writing undoubtedly through bitter experience, asserts that "it's their way of showing you're welcome, by making you drunk". Accordingly, the hall was the largest room in the castle and the most grandly appointed, with a capacious fire-basket prominent, either in the centre of the floor, as at Bothwell and Doune, or more commonly incorporated within a side or end wall. At one of the noblest state rooms of any private castle in Scotland, the Great Hall of Earl Patrick Stewart's palace at Kirkwall, there are not one but two huge fireplaces for warming the assembled company.

The centrepiece of the hall was the "hie burde", the high table, possibly set upon a slightly raised wooden platform, or dais, thereby accentuating the elevated status of the lord and his immediate entourage seated thereon. The remainder sat at side-tables around the hall below the dais. The lord alone was seated on a fine high-backed chair of state – hence the dignity of "chairman" and the invitation to "take the chair". An elaborate cloth of estate may have been suspended over or behind the chair, so emphasising the lofty station of its occupant. All others sat on benches, though some of the womenfolk may have been allowed individual stools covered with cushions. Other furniture included a chest or two, in which the napery, or table-linen, and other items were stored, and a cupboard (literally "a table for cups") where the lord's finest plate was displayed. This came in time to be put on show in aumbries, or wall-cupboards, and there are many fine aumbries to be seen, including a particularly elaborate one at Dirleton.

Meal times were occasions of ceremony and ritual, as much for lowly gentlemen as for great noblemen. One visitor recalls dining at a knight's house "who had many servants to attend him, that brought in his meate with their heads covered with blew caps". A contemporary of Earl Patrick Stewart's notes that "before dinner and supper there were three trumpeters that sounded still until the meat of the first service was set at table

and similarly at the second service and consequently after the Grace". The servants and musicians operated from the opposite end of the hall to the dais. Here was normally a timber screen which served both to close off the service area and to reduce draughts coming through the hall doorway. The service area is called the screens passage and in some cases may have had a gallery above where the minstrels played.

Thomas Kirke's headache might easily have been brought on as much by the musical accompaniment as by the alcohol. "Musick they have," he felt constrained to write, "but not the harmony of the sphears, but loud terrene noises, like the bellowing of beasts; the loud bagpipe is their chief delight." No timber screens with galleries over now survive (excepting Craigievar, in Grampian, in the care of the National Trust for Scotland), though the marks of where they have been affixed to the side walls are frequently visible. Two Victorian reconstructions at the Great Halls of Edinburgh and Doune convey the impression well enough. Where the screens passage has been constructed in stone, as at the Great Hall in Linlithgow Palace, both the serving hatches and the minstrels' gallery can be seen. The gallery within Sir James Hamilton's hall in Craignethan Castle is still remarkably intact.

Furnishings graced the hall, both to add a measure of colour and to further reduce cold and draughts. Brightly coloured worsteds draped against the walls gradually gave way to rich tapestries from the Low Countries. Cushions mellowed the icy cold of the stone window seats and the flagged floor was strewn with rushes of bent grass mixed with scented herbs in an effort to counteract the

unhygienic "flyes and other fylthe". The hastily discarded pikes of the fleeing Scots upon the battlefield of Pinkie (1547) were said to have resembled "a wood of staves strewed on the ground like rushes in a chamber". Later on, rugs and woven rush mats were introduced, and eventually carpets.

All these furnishings have long since rotted or otherwise disappeared from the halls of our Scottish castles and our sole legacy is but the cold stone shell making our appreciation of daily life in the medieval household that much more hard to comprehend. We are left to stare musingly into the bare fireplace, the wall-cupboard and closet, and through the stone-seated dais window that once brought sunshine and much needed ventilation to the high table, to picture in the mind's eye the contemporary scene.

As the medieval period drew to a close and with it the old feudal order, so lords felt a compelling desire for increased comfort and seclusion. They came to grace the hall with their presence far less frequently, preferring the quiet and intimacy of the smaller private chambers adjacent. The hall, in both size and scale, declined from being the centrepiece of the castle and in time became the simple entrance lobby it is today. By way of compensation, the private chambers grew in importance. Only in the royal palaces and baronial castles did the Great Hall continue to play a central role on prestigious occasions, as the Great Hall at Edinburgh continues to do to this day, but by the end of the medieval period in the castles of the humbler lords and lairds, the old hall had given way to the more familiar family dining-room.

The fireplace in John Carsewell's great chamber at sixteenth-century Carnasserie Castle.

The kitchen within Elcho Castle. Note, in particular, the brick-lined bake-oven in the left ingle-neuk, a common feature throughout Scotland's castles. Hot coals from the main fire were placed inside and the door (now missing) closed until the bricks were well heated. The ashes were then swept out and the bread, cakes or whatever popped inside and left to bake without further attention. After baking, the cooling oven was used to dry herbs, even firewood.

Second in importance to the hall was the **great chamber**, frequently termed the "chalmer of dais" on account of its position beyond the upper end of the hall, as at Dirleton, or perhaps above it, like Crookston. It was in effect a bed-sitting-room, frugally furnished with a bed or beds, a chair and side-table, a chest or two containing clothes and other valuables. The furnishings would have been akin to those in the adjacent hall. This chamber served originally as a haven of peace for the lord and his most intimate companions from the noise and bustle of the hall, but it came increasingly to be favoured as a living-room, where meals were

regularly taken, and a greater degree of entertainment pursued. It gradually assumed an importance greater than the hall and accordingly grew in size and sophistication. By the mid-sixteenth century, a nobleman's lodging might have assumed a quite complex arrangement taking in a sequence of three or more principal rooms, hall, outer or great chamber, inner chamber, perhaps a study, such as can be seen at the 4th Earl of Atholl's new building at Balvenie Castle, erected about 1550. All were reception rooms, graded according to the rank of those being received. The least distinguished were restricted to the hall, which served also as the dining-room; the outer chamber was the ancestor of the drawing-room; the inner chamber was the bedchamber.

Other rooms of significance within the castle included the **chapel** and the **gallery**. The former is not always distinguishable, but most lords would have ensured there was separate provision to allow for private prayers and devotion, as we can see at Doune. A particularly grand chapel was incorporated into the mighty thirteenth-century Kildrummy Castle. The gallery, a recreation room, made its appearance late on in the Middle Ages. Its origin is obscure but it may have grown from the timber balconies projecting out from the castle wall where fresh air and exercise were taken in inclement weather. Traces of such balconies can be seen at Craigmillar and Linlithgow. During the cultured and enlightened Jacobean Age, the gallery came into its own as a showpiece in the lord's castle, where his finest possessions were displayed and his family portraits hung. Newark, on the Clyde Estuary, and Rowallan possess good examples.

The greater part of a lord's wealth came from rents and dues which were paid largely in kind, not always in cash and much of the castle's accommodation was taken up with kitchens, stores and other service offices. This relative abundance of food and provisions sustained the ceremony and hospitality that went on in hall and chamber and was an integral part of the feudal way of life. **Kitchens** were furnished with boards, or tables, on which the food was prepared; and were dominated by the massive fireplace, in some instances more than one, on which the cauldrons, skillets, pots and pans frothed and bubbled, spat and stewed. Fish and meat were frequently smoked in the chimney flue above the fire, whilst salt, important as a preservative, was kept dry by being stored in a vessel placed close to the flames, often in an aumbry alongside. The enormous breadth of

The serving hatches in the kitchen at Doune Castle, linking with the great hall across the passage (see illustration on page 10). Such openings are not uncommon, though by no means as grand except in the greatest of castles. The projecting stone corbel on the left, one of two, supported a shelf upon which the scullions, or kitchen domestics, stored the pots, pans and other utensils.

some fireplaces allowed the "turnbrochie" space to turn the roasting spit, and a bread oven is frequently to be found tucked into one corner. A stone channel bringing fresh water into the kitchen, and a slopsink and drain taking waste matter out are common features.

Adjacent to the kitchen were the **pantry** (from the French "paneterie", bread store) and **buttery** or wine cellar (from the French "bouteillerie", bottle store), the latter often recognisable by a separate stair linking it with the lord's chamber above. Other miscellaneous **storerooms** were clustered around, with iron hooks and rings suspended from their stone vaults on which flitches of pork and the like were hung. The remainder of the produce was stored in barrels. In some cases, Auchindoun for example, perishable foods were kept in a cold-store hewn out of the rock in the floor of the cellar, a sort of medieval refrigerator. The staple diet of bread and ale for the lower orders in the household required the separate provision of a **brewhouse** and **bakehouse**. The nobility generally drank imported wines.

The Scottish castle was rarely without suitable **prison** accommodation, for the feudal lord had responsibility for law and order ("pit and gallows") within his barony. Imprisonment was not then a form of punishment in itself but more a means of temporary confinement until such time as the accused could be brought to trial. Nonetheless, these "pits" were almost without exception dark, dank holes, often devoid of light, air or sanitation. The miscreants were pushed in through a trap in the ceiling and left to reflect on their wrong-doing, some to end their miserable days therein. In some castles, Cardoness for example, the prison

The voluminous vaults beneath the hall and chamber block built by the Halyburtons at Dirleton Castle in the later fourteenth century. The payment by the lord's tenants of rentals and other dues in kind, not cash, necessitated substantial storage accommodation for perishables and other produce.

Wooden platter (fourteenth century) from Threave Castle, used for every day tableware.

accommodation comprised two chambers one above the other, the lower grim and stark in contrast to the better appointed one above with its more acceptable lighting, ventilation and privy. Even in its treatment of wrong-doers medieval society paid due regard to rank and station. The siting of prisons within the castle is not without interest, even significance. At Dirleton, the prison and "pit" are directly beneath the private chapel; elsewhere it is not uncommon to find them tucked beneath the hall or chamber where the lord literally had the "devil" beneath his feet. At Blackness on the Forth estuary, in use as a state prison as recently as the eighteenth century, there is a particularly grim pit lacking all amenities save the ebb and flow of the tide "slopping out" twice daily. The most intriguing prison is the bottle dungeon at St Andrews, where, says John Knox, "many of God's children were imprisoned". As recently as 1916, David Kirkwood, a "Red

The patchwork of doorways and windows opening off the courtyard at Craigmillar Castle. The castle of a great lord had to serve as court, hotel and barrack as well as private residence, and extensive accommodation was required not just for the lord's family but for his household and guests. At Craigmillar, these quarters are built of stone and survive; at many other castles they were of timber and are now the subject of archaeological enquiry only.

Clydesider", was incarcerated in one of the medieval "pits" at Edinburgh Castle. He later wrote that he felt like "a done man" when he was thrown down.

The prison, kitchens, bakehouses, brewhouses and other service offices like the **stables**, **laundry**, **porter's lodge** and **fuel store** required to be staffed and managed by a substantial retinue of servants, many of whom were accommodated within the castle. The size of household, of course, varied considerably, depending on the status of its master. The most senior members of the household – the constable, steward and so forth – were accommodated in their own quarters, the remainder slept in the hall, pantry or wherever. The lord's personal servant slept beside his master, perhaps on a truckle bed, on the floor or maybe in the corridor outside his chamber. As time went by it was considered preferential to distance the majority of the household as far as possible from the principal apartments. A lower or "laich" hall for their exclusive use came to be provided, as at Tantallon, and the age of the common feast had

given way to the era of the private dinner-party. Personal servants came to be accommodated in closets adjacent to those of their masters and mistresses, corridors were more frequently used, and the introduction of the back-stair for the use of domestic staff contributed to the increased privacy of the host and his guests. The main stair now assumed a greater dignity within the overall design, and broad, elegantly treated scale-and-platt staircases, as at Crichton, ousted the old, constricted spiral steps.

Hospitality was a major feature of medieval society, particularly amongst the aristocracy, and the rendering of hospitality to another lord, who would be accompanied by a goodly number of his own household, imposed additional pressure on the host finding accommodation for them all. Separate lodgings had to be provided, all adding to the size and complexity of the castle.

The medieval household was certainly a mobile one. In addition to enjoying other noblemen's hospitality, many major barons possessed several estates scattered throughout the realm and, in

The stable-block at Crichton Castle, with the stalls at ground level and ostlers' quarters over. Note the horseshoe-shaped over-light above the doorway.

order that they could collect their food-rents, found it expedient to transfer from one estate to another, and from one castle to another so that they could consume their dues. Most of the household moved with its lord, leaving a small staff behind to clean and prepare the castle for its master's return. Along with the household went most of the contents of the castle, in a baggage train. As a consequence, furniture was limited and largely dismountable for easy transportation. The main items, the "boards" or tables, were of the trestle variety; the lord's canopied bed was taken too; much of the remainder, tableware, linen, furnishings and valuables, was stowed in the numerous iron-bound wooden cists, or chests, and taken forward. It was not unknown even for the casement windows with their precious glass panes to be taken out and packed, and temporarily replaced with fixed wooden shutters.

The passing of the Middle Ages saw a gradual transition to a more settled, static society. From about the beginning of the sixteenth century, rents from the estates came increasingly to be paid in money, not kind, obviating the need to journey from castle to castle and reducing substantially the requirement for voluminous storage space. More and better furniture pieces became a feature of the castle. Great solid dining-tables on finely carved legs took the place of the more basic trestle-boards; wooden benches made way for more comfortable, upholstered chairs; beds became increasingly more ornate; cupboards were no longer simple "boards for cups" but the more substantial tall cabinets familiar to us today. Basic amenities were greatly improved including the better location of the kitchen closer to the dining-room. Even the day of the humble privy was at an end as this hitherto somewhat crude and draughty chute carrying soil down to the base of the castle walls – the major cause of all those "flyes and other filthe" – was abandoned in favour of the infinitely more acceptable and hygienic closed stool. More agreeably, we see the emergence, as at Edzell, of the grand, formal garden landscape as an important adjunct to the castle. The age of the fortress was passing; the residence had come into its own.

THE CASTLE AS FORTRESS

"Thate daye thai schote downe all the battellyne and caiphouse of the seytowre; and all this daye tha schate upone the easte parte of the castell . . . at the hall and chapell, and dislogid us of that parte be downputting of the ruffis and sklatis."
(Eye-witness account during the siege of St Andrews Castle, 1546)

THE MEDIEVAL CASTLE was a fortified residence and its builder was called upon to provide for his lord's accommodation needs within a framework of sound defence. Both requirements were the subject of continual modification throughout the medieval period, the former on account of increasing desires for domestic comfort, the latter out of sheer necessity as the technology of warfare improved.

The first castle builders used earth and timber in the main as their construction materials. Attacks on their castles consisted primarily of bombardment by incendiary devices closely followed by a headlong assault by soldiers on foot and knights on horseback. The garrison took comfort from the height advantage afforded by the high bank and palisade, relying upon wet hides draped over roof and wall to reduce the risk of fire. On occasion, castles were blockaded; hence the need for ample storage space and a fresh water supply, usually from a draw-well, within the castle walls.

The experience of the western nations in the Middle East during the Crusades brought about a considerable change in castle architecture. The mighty stone defences around the towns and castles of the Levant were far more sophisticated than anything they had yet encountered. Against these formidable walls their own siege machines were ineffective, their massed assaults easily beaten off. As the knights returned home they rethought their ideas on siege warfare and the defensive capabilities of their castles.

An important consequence of this revolution in warfare was a preference for castles of stone, better

able to withstand the onslaught from heavy siege artillery. This consisted primarily of ballistas, mangonels and trebuchets, machines capable of hurling considerable weights and missiles at a static object using the principles of tension, torsion and counterpoise. Their high trajectory meant they were more effective at the upper levels of a castle, damaging roofs and breaching wall-tops.

Equally ingenious machines and measures were brought to bear against the lower parts of the walls. The battering-ram was more effective against the most vulnerable part of a castle, its entrance doorway. Elsewhere along the defensive circuit breaches were made by sappers, or miners, hewing their way through the masonry, as the Norsemen did at Rothesay in 1230, or burrowing like moles through the rock beneath, as the Earl of Arran's men attempted to do at St Andrews Castle in 1546. Both the surface sapper and those operating the battering-ram were protected overhead by a mobile cover, known as a "sow", which was pushed against the walls and deflected any

A castle under siege (thirteenth century). The besiegers assail the stronghold with heavy artillery, battering ram and sappers hewing at the wall base; the besieged conduct their defence from the wall head with a combination of brute force and ingenuity.

Caerlaverock was cunning often fatal, tides of the Sol

In addition to making terrain, builders of stone those artificial defensive their predecessors well. banks outside the castle encumbrances to assailar foot or attempting to b towers and "sows" b particularly if the encir water.

Besides being lofty an designed in such a way easy as possible for the consideration of the b the enormous destruct siege engines. In a machines as far remove the fighting platform battlements, was give parapet, pierced by e were known as crenell as merlons which tog This allowed the def

The mine at St Andrews Castle.

An English spy's somewhat distorted perspective of Caerlaverock Castle, drawn between 1563 and 1566, showing the defensive features then in existence. The portcullis and drawbridge are now gone but evidence of their existence is still detectable in the fabric of the gatehouse.

The two-leafed iron yett, or gate, within the pend at Balvenie Castle, intended to withstand an onslaught from a battering-ram.

open. If the door were burnt or broken up, the yett would hold and the defenders could shoot out between its bars.

The strategic siting of castles and the provision of external ditches and banks could make an entrance well-nigh unreachable. At Dirleton and Dunstaffnage, the main entrance was in effect high above ground level and at Caerlaverock, at least by the fifteenth century, there were two broad, water-filled ditches to overcome. The bridges that were constructed over these obstacles to allow easy access in times of peace were, of necessity, fitted with devices which could readily negate their use to an enemy. Most bridges

Great oak timbers from the bridge formerly crossing the inner moat at Caerlaverock Castle, discovered during archaeological investigations in the 1960s. Excavation showed they belonged to two bridges, and dendro-chronological dating proved that the first bridge had been constructed about 1277 with its replacement being built a century later. The timbers are still beneath the water surface.

The drawbridge, a restoration built in 1976, being raised into the gatehouse of the fifteenth-century artillery fortification at Threave Castle.

incorporated a movable section, which could either be rolled back into the castle or, more usually, lifted up and back. In the latter case, the raised section of bridge became an invaluable extra barrier across the entrance, complementing the door and portcullis.

No medieval bridges have survived complete. All that can be seen today are the shapes of the masonry features built to accommodate them: the recess in the gatehouse which housed the raised portion; the "rainures", or vertical slots for the gaffs of the drawbridge or other apertures for the hoisting mechanism; the deep pit immediately inside the gatehouse housing the back part of a

The need for security throughout the castle is well demonstrated at Kildrummy Castle. Left, a square slot indicates the position of a timber draw-bar securing the door linking the Earl of Mar's great hall and chamber; right, a window in the great hall has holes for iron cross-bars and a square slot for another draw-bar securing the shutters.

lifting-bridge of the counterpoise variety. The early bridges, like the thirteenth-century bridge across the inner moat at Caerlaverock and its late fourteenth-century successor (excavated in the 1960s; the present bridge is a modern one) were most probably of all-timber construction. Later bridges could well have incorporated more in the way of stonework. Nonetheless, no matter what precautions were taken (and in the early tower-houses entrances were often placed at an upper storey reached only by retractable ladders (see page 48)), the point of entrance into a castle was undoubtedly its weakest point and it is not unusual to discover a small box-machicolation, or bretasche, placed, as at Bothwell or Corgarff, directly over the entry.

A further defensive precaution was the so-called "murder-hole", an opening in the ceiling of the entrance passage through which missiles could be dropped upon assailants who had broken through the outer barriers. These can take the form of simple holes punched through the vault of the entrance passage, as at Dirleton and Cardoness, the mid fifteenth-century home of Gilbert McCulloch. A more sophisticated provision was installed at the fourteenth-century tower-houses at David's Tower, in Edinburgh Castle, and at Craigmillar, where the entrance vestibule has been ceiled with a movable timber decking. Such openings may not, of course, have contributed solely to the defensive well-being of the castle; they may equally have served to facilitate the lifting or lowering of goods and furniture.

The garrison's defence of a castle did not necessarily end with the breaching of the main curtain or enclosing wall. Sliding draw-bars securing inner doors, arrow-slits, or gun-loops in the later castles, and other assorted security devices were placed at strategic points within the enclosure. This was particularly the case at the great thirteenth-century castles where individual elements in the building complex were designed in such a way that they could be separately defended even though the outer defences had fallen. At Bothwell, in addition to the curtain-wall defences, each of the towers ranged about the courtyard could be independently defended to a greater or lesser extent. The donjon, or keep, housing the lord's principal apartments was understandably afforded the greatest measure of protection with its own water-filled moat and drawbridge, arrow-slits, box-machicolation, portcullis and an awkward zig-zagged entrance passage. The ancillary towers were less well secured, though the now-largely demolished rectangular tower along the eastern stretch of curtain-wall had its own drawbridge. The arrangement at Bothwell is highly sophisticated and, indeed, may have been inspired as much by the lord's desire to display his exalted position as by any concern he may have had regarding his protection. Elsewhere the same ideas are executed in a more humble fashion.

The preference for heavy siege bombardment and blockade necessitated the presence of ample storage space for provisions within the enclosure, together with a water supply, normally in the form of a well. This is not to say that buildings were specifically erected for such a purpose; rather, this eventuality was taken into account when assessing the domestic requirements of the household as a whole. In wartime anything goes, as the unfortunate experience of Sir Nigel Bruce and his defending garrison at Kildrummy in 1306 reveals. In their attempt to get in as many essential supplies as possible, they filled the hall with corn. All went well for a time, the besieging force failing to make any impact upon the castle walls or upon the garrison within – until the treacherous black-smith, Osborne, set light to the corn forcing the inmates to surrender forthwith.

Large and costly assaults upon castles may have presented the greatest spectacles but they were not readily entered into by the besieging force. A prolonged bombardment by the distant heavy siege engines coupled with a blockade of the castle, thereby denying the garrison access to food and other provisions, was unquestionably the preferred approach. The retrospective experiences of Scots and English at Bothwell Castle at the outset of the Wars of Independence were markedly different. In 1298–99, following a tedious blockade of fourteen months, the Scots stormed the castle and captured it, finding Stephen de Brampton, the garrison commander, one of few remaining alive, the remainder having perished either during the bombardment or through famine and disease. In 1301, Edward I of England recaptured the castle in under one month, possibly on account of the greater arsenal of siege machines under his control.

Edward I's obsession with mighty siege machines can be well illustrated at the siege of Stirling Castle in 1304, one of the classics of all medieval sieges. The main siege (which included in its arsenal an engine nicknamed "Bothwell") lasted three months, whereafter the garrison, along with their constable, Sir William Oliphant, surrendered. However, as Sir Walter de Bedewyne wrote at the time: "the King wills it that none of his people enter the castle till it is struck with his 'War Wolf' and that those within the castle defend themselves from the said 'War Wolf' as best they can". Evidently most eager to demonstrate the capabilities of his latest war-machine, Edward made quite a spectacle of the ensuing display, assembling his queen and her ladies in a watching-chamber so that they might have a grandstand view.

This gruesome stone face from Caerlaverock Castle, doubtless placed in a prominent position on the outside of the curtain-wall, silently threatens those "wha daur meddle wi' me", on behalf of its Maxwell lord within.

THE FIRST CASTLES

*"There lived in Wyre in the Orkneys a Norwegian called
Kolbein Hruga [who] had a fine stone castle built there; it
was a safe stronghold."*
(Orkneyinga Saga, c. 1145)

A MEDIEVAL CASTLE was essentially a creation of the feudal system, by which vassals held their lands from superior lords in return for military service. The roots of feudalism are to be found in the disintegration of Charlemagne's empire in the ninth century. The almost constant, often brutal, warring, or feuding, which followed as the power of the old kingships waned and as disputed territories were fought over, forced vassals to seek the protection of their superiors. The need for strong defences was paramount among the warrior aristocracy.

The feudal system was radically transformed by the Normans in the tenth and eleventh centuries. They established a firm central authority at the head, and beneath, at local level, the holding of land was inextricably linked to a responsibility for law and order. Those holding knights' fees, or feus, enjoyed baronial jurisdiction, known as "sake, soke, toll, team and infangenthief", together with "pit and gallows". The castle was created not solely for reasons of defence; it became a symbol of lordship, a place of local government and centre for administration and justice. In times of peace it served both as the private residence of its lord, family and retainers, and also as a public court, to which vassals were obliged to come for redress in civil and criminal causes. In times of war the castle became not simply a place of safety but also a gathering point for the feudal host as the lord's vassals fulfilled their obligations of military service to their superior.

The castle first appeared in Scotland in the twelfth century. It was introduced not just by one foreign

Norseman and Norman. These two warriors, both carved from walrus ivory in the twelfth century, portray the two races that introduced castles to Scotland. Opposite, a castle or rook piece from the chess set discovered on the Isle of Lewis in 1831 and most probably made in a Scandinavian workshop. On this page, a knight, perhaps a depiction of Hercules, on a comb discovered at Jedburgh Abbey in Scotland's Border country in 1984 and thought to have been made in Norman England. (*Chess-piece reproduced by kind permission of the Royal Museum of Scotland*)

29

element, the Normans, but also by their non-feudal, non-Latinised kinsmen, the Norsemen, for Norse earls had controlled much of the north and west, chiefly Shetland, Orkney, Caithness, the Hebrides and Argyll, since the early ninth century. Though they were forced to surrender their western territories and Caithness to the increasingly dominant kings of Scots by the mid thirteenth century, the Northern Isles were not formally relinquished until a further two hundred years had elapsed.

Duffus Castle, the perfect model of a Norman motte and bailey castle in state care, erected about 1150 by a "soldier of fortune" Freskin, founder of the House of Moray.

The motte-castle of the bishops of Dol, in Brittany, as depicted on the Bayeux Tapestry. Although a stylisation, the flat-topped mound is clearly apparent surrounded by its ditch and counterscarp. The timber tower, palisade and flying bridge are features which have nowhere survived in any of Scotland's examples except as archaeological features. The Stewarts of Scotland, who built numerous motte-castles, were descended from the stewards of the bishops of Dol.

The Normans, on the other hand, came to Scotland not as invaders but initially at the invitation of her kings. Certainly there were mailed Norman knights serving with the king at least as early as the reign of Macbeth in the 1050s, but it was not until the youngest of the sons of Malcolm III and St Margaret, David, came into possession of southern Scotland about the year 1113, whilst his elder brother, Alexander I, was king of Scots, that Normans first settled on Scottish soil. This colonisation, primarily but not exclusively of Anglo-Norman stock, continued for the next century or so, until only at the death of David's grandson, William the Lion, in 1214, was the process of foreign settlement largely complete. The twelfth-century monarchs were instrumental in bringing Scotland out of the Celtic twilight and fully into the Continental sphere of mainland Europe.

This radical change was not achieved entirely without antipathy and bloodshed. Certain strongly Celtic areas attempted to resist, like Moray in the north of the country. This ancient earldom was ruthlessly suppressed by David I and certain native landowners dispossessed following their abortive rebellion of 1130. The forfeited lands were granted to the newcomers. One, Freskin, an adventurous Fleming already peaceably settled in Strathbrock (now Uphall) in West Lothian, received the lands of Duffus, and the castle he chose to build there still rises from the Laich o' Moray "like a boss on a buckler". Duffus Castle remained a fortress-residence for over five hundred years and, not surprisingly, during that time it underwent substantial change. The most radical was the replacement of the original wooden buildings by ones of stone from the fourteenth century on, and yet, despite this wholesale remodelling, Duffus remains the model of a Norman motte and bailey castle in state care.

The chief element was the elevated, flat-topped mound, the **motte** (the Norman word for "mound"), upon which were erected the principal residential buildings of the lord, normally constructed of wood and clay. The height of the motte, coupled with its steeply sloping sides, comprised the basic defence, suitably reinforced by a timber palisade, or protective fence, around the perimeter of the summit, and by a ditch, possibly water-filled, encircling the base. Ancillary buildings, like the chapel, bakehouse, brewhouse and stables, were grouped around the motte, often within the **bailey**, or courtyard, not normally as elevated as the motte but raised above timber, upon Freskin's motte at Duffus, or Earl Duncan's motte at Huntly, and within Robert Croc's ring-work at Crookston. But Kolbein Hruga and his fellow Norsemen were not feudal lords. They were, nevertheless, not slow in appreciating the contribution of the castle to the success their southern kinsmen achieved in conquest throughout Europe. The Norse earls themselves were no novices to conquest and its consequent and continuing requirement to maintain a grip over their new subjects. The Norsemen were no doubt ready and eager to adopt this effective instrument of subjugation, adapting it to serve their own particular needs, and they can hardly have failed to be aware of its existence for there was frequent contact between Scotland and her Norse neighbours both during their many hostile encounters, particularly along the western seaboard, as well as in more peaceful ways.

An instance of peaceful contact was the marriage in about 1150 of Harald Maddadson, Earl of Caithness, to Affrica, a daughter of Earl Duncan of Fife, whose son we have seen was probably responsible for the imposing motte and bailey castle at Huntly. One of Harald's kinsmen,

perhaps Harald h
of Old Wick, on
North Sea betwe
or geos, a little s
ruined shell of t
has four unvault
first-floor doorwa
the few window
ledges, supportin
featureless, and
the storeroom at
principal apartme
chambers for the
family above. S
tower, upon th
grass-grown foun
which though une
contemporaneous
probably twelfth c

The two castles
belong to differen
not, but there car
tradition. And
beckoned, so Nor
improved upon tha

the surrounding land and protected likewise by a palisade and ditch.

There are over 250 motte-castles in Scotland. Some, like Freskin's Duffus and the motte and bailey castle at Huntly, built on his Strathbogie estate in the later twelfth century probably by Earl Duncan of Fife, a Celtic earl who had readily embraced the new order, have subsequently been built upon by castle buildings of stone and lime. The majority, like those at Druchtag and Coulter, ceased to serve as baronial centres (known as *caputs*) at an early date and survive today merely as grassy mounds, their timber buildings long since gone and their ditches now silted up. That at Lincluden College has been terraced and incorporated into a later medieval formal garden scheme.

Not all mottes were artificially constructed of made-up earth, for the hilly terrain of much of Scotland enabled certain lords to utilise natural outcrops commanding outstanding views, thereby saving them considerable expense. Such is likely to have been the case at Urquhart Castle where there may have been a castle from the time of William the Lion. Here the natural hour-glass configurations of the rock readily lent themselves to being formed into a motte and bailey. Its promontory, projecting into the deep, peat-blackened waters of Loch Ness from its steep north-western shore, was of crucial importance to the castle's role in the policing of this remote and lawless region. Above all, three of the most important castles of the realm, the royal residences at Dumbarton, Edinburgh and Stirling, were sited upon well-nigh impregnable extinct volcanoes.

Stirling Castle clings to the summit of a long-extinct volcano rising from the flood-plain of the Forth valley.

31

the Rouen district of Normandy, John built a remarkable stone castle about the year 1240 upon a craggy knoll on his land right in the heart of the realm. His motive in so doing can only have been an earnest desire to display his wealth and status. Furthermore, he elected to imitate the fashion of castle-building adopted by his patron's father, Enguerrand, lord of Coucy in northern France, with a great round tower, housing the principal apartments, dominating a courtyard encircled by a high curtain-wall strongly defended with round towers of lesser girth.

The castle that recalls Coucy most closely, however, is Bothwell, built beside the Clyde about the middle of the century by Walter of Moray, a descendant of Freskin, lord of Duffus. The full scheme of building was never completed, perhaps

The fifteenth-century stone fortress-residence of Sir John Stewart of Darnley at Crookston Castle stands within a defensive earthwork dating to Sir Robert Croc's time in the late twelfth century.

St Margaret's Chapel in Edinburgh Castle, the sole surviving structure from King David I's royal fortress. This somewhat enigmatic building, though now free-standing, may originally have been part of a much larger, residential keep placed on the far, northern side – the highest part of the Castle Rock.

Mottes, whether man-made or natural, we means the only form of castle used. Inc Scotland they may have been the exceptio than the rule, for by far the greater nu found in areas like Galloway which were from the centre of royal power. There is ar total absence of mottes in Lothian (wh instance, was Freskin's castle at Strathbroc in Tweeddale, where the process of infe was comprehensively achieved at an earl This suggests that the incoming Anglo-N and those native land-holders who had er the new order had no need of such strong d in those areas. Quite what form their *caputs* not known, but there has fortuitously surv Crookston a twelfth-century earthwork cas

Coucy-le-Chateau (Aisne), in France, built by Duke Enguerrand III, the Scots' queen's father, in the 1220s (as sketched by Thomas Ross in the late nineteenth century before its destruction by German soldiers in the Great War). Considered one of the grandest military structures in Europe, its planned arrangement of a polygonal curtain-wall, with round towers projecting out from the angles and a mighty donjon, or main tower, dominating all, may have directly influenced the form of several of Scotland's great thirteenth-century castles, among them Dirleton, Bothwell and Kildrummy.

Bothwell Castle from the air. The original scheme was intended to take in the ground in the foreground, but in the event the stone footings were never taken any higher. The mighty donjon of Walter of Moray, on the right, was so badly damaged in the Wars of Independence that it was never fully repaired by the new lords, the Black Douglases, but largely replaced by new buildings, which today form the greater part of this outstanding ruin.

Bothwell Castle donjon:
details

a wall-walk
b zig-zag entrance passage
c doorway
d upper floors
e mural passage
f hall window
g spiral stair
h latrine with arrow-slit below
i vault ribs
j octagonal central pier

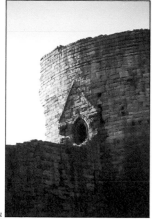

a

h

b

d

e

i

c

f

g

j

being interrupted by the outbreak of the Wars of Independence in 1296. By then, only the foundation courses of the extensive curtain-wall had been laid, the main effort having gone into the construction of the immense great tower, or *donjon* (the word has since been corrupted into *dungeon*, with an altogether different connotation), justly described as "the grandest and most accomplished piece of mediaeval secular architecture in Scotland". Though not quite so massive as that at Coucy, by Scottish standards it represents a spectacular display of feudal pride by one of the foremost barons of the realm and must have placed a severe strain upon the resources both of finance and manpower that even such a magnate as Walter of Moray was able to call upon.

Herbert de Maxwell, a member of one of Dumfriesshire's most notable families, came into possession of his estates in 1266, including the lands of Caerlaverock beside the Solway Firth and facing the high peaks of the English Lakeland. There he chose to build his castle, one of the most impressive of all the castles in Britain, about 1277. Much of what we see today dates from the fourteenth century and later, for the place suffered considerable damage in the Wars of Independence. Nonetheless, sufficient survives of Herbert's original residence to show that it was a most formidable, and imposing, strength. It shares with Dirleton and Bothwell the lofty curtain-wall, but here the lord's main apartments are situated within the gatehouse complex and not placed elsewhere within the enceinte, or enclosure.

A contemporary of Herbert de Maxwell, Alexander the Stewart (1241–82), elected to build likewise, it would appear, at Dundonald, in the heart of his Kyle estates. Alexander's forebears were men with impeccable Norman credentials. Before the Conquest they had served as stewards to the bishops of Dol in Brittany (whose motte-castle is depicted on the Bayeux Tapestry). One of their number, Alan son of Flaad, crossed to England with the Conqueror's son, Henry I, about 1100 and profited greatly from his regal contacts. Alan's third son, Walter, took service with David I about 1136, becoming stewart of the royal household, a post which soon became hereditary. The Stewart came to hold considerable estates in southern Scotland, including Kyle in Ayrshire. The mighty courtyard-castle erected at Dundonald by Alexander in the later thirteenth century was largely dismantled and incorporated into an equally grandiose tower-house by his great-grandson, Robert, who became the first monarch of the House of Stewart in 1371.

The building of such costly residences was not the prerogative solely of the secular nobility. Bishop Roger of St Andrews erected a fine castle beside his cathedral about 1200 and it is not improbable that the earliest masonry existing within the Fore Tower is part of his residence. The Bishop's Palace at Kirkwall, in Norse-held Orkney, was substantially remodelled in the sixteenth century but the alterations have not masked the fine early medieval masonry on the ground floor, possibly of late twelfth-century date – the undercroft, or cellar, beneath the hall in which the great King Haakon IV died in 1263 following his defeat at the Battle of Largs.

Considerations over and above feudal pride exercised the minds of those lords holding lands in areas remote from the centre of royal power. For the Earl of Mar, whose estates bordered the rebellious province of Moray, where trouble again broke out in 1228, a great stone castle was no luxury but a paramount necessity and the mighty stronghold he built at Kildrummy beside the River Don – "the noblest of northern castles" – gives proof of his overriding concern for security and a dominating countenance. The castle walls today are sadly more ruinous than we would wish and make analysis of its building history difficult. The original arrangement would seem to have mirrored, on a reduced scale, that at Walter of Moray's Bothwell, with the solid mass of the donjon at the rear of a polygonal curtain-wall punctured at intervals by projecting flanking towers, one of which doubtless housed the constable, or keeper of the castle. The mighty gatehouse tower appears not to have been an element in the original plan but was added at the beginning of the following century possibly on the orders of Edward I of England, whose son, Edward of Caernarvon, had captured the stronghold in 1306. If this is so, it is the sole surviving remnant of the handiwork of the "Hammer of the Scots" on Scottish soil; all trace of his recorded building activity at Linlithgow and Lochmaben having long since disappeared.

Throughout the reigns of the kings of peace, senior representatives of the most powerful of all Scotland's baronial families, the Comyns, were engaged upon the building of formidable castles on their northern estates. The Black Comyn, possibly Alexander, Earl of Buchan (1244–89), was responsible for Balvenie, or Mortlach, as it was then known, in Glen Fiddich. The Red Comyn, John, as lord of Lochaber, built that at Inverlochy, guarding the southern end of the Great Glen, about 1275. The same John, as lord of Badenoch,

This late eighteenth-century engraving of Kildrummy Castle (far right) shows the great donjon still standing almost to full height (it collapsed in 1805). A visitor, writing in 1725, described this tower as having five dome-vaulted floors, and at the apex of each vault was an "eye" through which water was hoisted from a draw-well in the base (see illustration below). The tower in the centre, still standing much like that today, is called the Warden's Tower, the lodging of the Earl of Mar's constable, or keeper. Note on its left three tall and slender lancet windows formerly lighting the east, altar end of the lord's chapel.

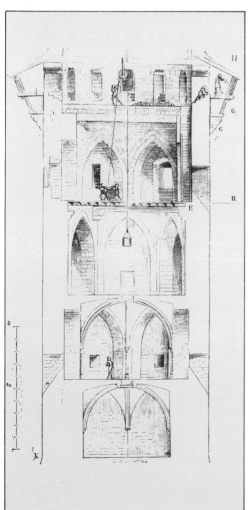

left
A section through one of the towers at Coucy-le-Chateau, by the nineteenth-century architect Viollet-le-Duc. The accommodation comprises a storage basement with three residential floors above and a fighting platform at the top.

The provision for lifting heavy goods recalls what the visitor to Kildrummy Castle in 1725 witnessed.

below
A stretch of wall-walk at Inverlochy Castle. This communicating passage, no doubt originally covered over for the better protection of the garrison stationed at the wall-head, can be traced around the entire defensive circuit.

also had a castle at his *caput* there, Ruthven, near Kingussie, since obliterated and replaced ultimately by a Hanoverian barracks (see page 75). In addition, another strategically sited castle, at Urquhart on Loch Ness, passed into the hands of the Red Comyn following the death of Alan Durward, Earl of Atholl, and brother-in-law of Alexander II (to whom he was hereditary "doorward", or royal bodyguard) in either 1268 or 1275. Either magnate could have been responsible for refashioning the original twelfth-century timber castle in stone.

Conditions in the west of the country were, if anything, more unstable, for the seaboard, both islands and mainland alike, though nominally under the authority of the two kingdoms of Scotland and Norway, was in point of fact controlled by two independent-minded princelings. The isles of Man, Skye and Lewis were under the sway of the kings of Man; the remainder, from Gigha to the Uists, were held by the descendants of Somerled (Norse for "summer voyager") who in the mid twelfth century had obtained the larger part of the lordship of the isles. These sons of Somerled held mainland (Scottish) lands also. Friction between the various parties was inevitable, though by the time of Alexander III's death the threat from Norway and Man had been removed.

The first island to fall into the Scottish king's hands was Bute, in the Firth of Clyde, some time before 1200. The Stewart came into possession, thereby adding to his already extensive land-holding across the Firth in the fiefs of Renfrew and Kyle. Whereas Walter the Stewart (1204–41) was content, apparently, to make do with timber castles on his mainland estates, at his *caput* on Bute, Rothesay, he constructed a great castle of stone. It comprised a circular curtain-wall of stone (sometimes called a shell-keep), 10 m high and 3 m thick, enclosing a courtyard 45 m across wherein were placed the domestic apartments and service offices, probably of timber construction. The four projecting round towers were added later in the century, and the gatehouse lodging not till the reign of James IV. The circular, uncomplicated form of the first castle at Rothesay recalls several important English castles, like Arundel. By coincidence, the latter came into the possession of a close relation of the Stewart, John FitzAlan, lord of Oswestry, about 1243, but whereas the FitzAlans, the senior line of the two,

The ruin of Rothesay Castle dominates the town in this painting by J Clark, dated 1824. The importance of water to communication on the western seaboard, even at this comparatively late date, is patently clear.
(*Reproduced by kind permission of the Royal Commission on the Ancient and Historical Monuments of Scotland*)

remained in England and became a great baronial family, as earls of Arundel, the Stewarts had elected to come north and, in the fullness of time, were rewarded with the crown of Scotland.

The Stewart's assessment of the uncertain political situation, leading him to invest in a stone castle, soon showed foresight, for Rothesay was attacked by a Norse raiding force in 1230. Unfortunately for the garrison within, and despite their stout resistance, "the Norwegians hewed the wall with axes" and ultimately gained entry, spilling much blood. The Norse withdrew shortly after but when King Haakon IV of Norway next returned, in 1263, and recaptured the castle, it provided the prelude to the final ceding of suzerainty of the Isles by the Norwegians to Scotland.

The sons of Somerled to the west of the Stewart – the MacDonalds of Islay and part of Kintyre; the MacDougalls of Lorn, Lismore, Mull, Coll and Tiree; and the lords of Garmoran (in the most northerly of the isles) – may have been men of ancient Irish stock but they showed little reluctance in embracing the institutions and architecture introduced into mainland Scotland by the foreign colonists. A remarkable group of castles, solidly built of stone and displaying characteristics which prove that their builders were far from ignorant of fashions current throughout western Europe, has survived within their former domains. Almost without exception they are perched upon rocky promontories hard by the sea or loch shore, reminding us of the overriding importance of water to communication. Each lord had a sizeable fleet of galleys at his disposal and a substantial tenantry scattered throughout his territory upon whom he could call at will.

The MacSweens were lords of Knapdale. One of their number, possibly Dugald, built himself a strong castle overlooking the eastern shore of the

Rothesay Castle from the air, highlighting its unique, circular form. The imposing gatehouse-block projecting into the water-filled moat on the left side and the rectangular chapel within the courtyard are later medieval additions to the original thirteenth-century core.

Castle Sween. Like Rothesay
Castle, later medieval
additions mask the otherwise
uncomplicated design of the
first castle.

sea-loch called Sween early in the century. Its high, quadrangular stone wall, over 2 m thick, encloses an area less than half the size of that at Rothesay, which today gives the impression of an open courtyard but which, in Dugald MacSween's time, would have been crowded with timber buildings, the traces of which can be seen in the curtain-wall, but whose form and plan are a mystery.

This may have been the same Dugald MacSween who built a castle of a quite different form at Skipness, a crucial location on the north-east coast of Kintyre guarding the confluence of Loch Fyne, Kilbrannan Sound and the Sound of Bute. Skipness, however, consisted not of a strong stone curtain-walled enclosure; instead, there were originally two free-standing stone structures, one a two-storey, oblong building, with a hall and chamber on the upper floor, the other a chapel. Neither would seem to have been particularly strong defensively. It is tempting to picture the two structures linked by a defensive perimeter wall, or palisade, of timber, enclosing a courtyard in which were other less significant buildings. Be this as it may, much of the first castle was swept away (the chapel was resited at some distance) and replaced by a far more defensible fortress towards the end of the thirteenth century, perhaps as a result of the worsening political situation with England, when the MacDonald lord of Islay entered into an alliance with Edward I of England to resist the expansionist aims of the MacDougall lord of Lorn.

Directly across the Kilbrannan Sound from Skipness stands Lochranza Castle, one of three medieval castles on the Island of Arran. To the casual eye it appears as a tower-house and typically late medieval. This is altogether misleading for the Montgomeries, who came into possession of north Arran in 1452, did not build a new fortress on their estate but adapted an existing construction, a castle which bears a striking resemblance to the first castle at Skipness and with which it must be contemporary. The builder of Lochranza is unknown to us; it is just possible that it was the same Dugald MacSween of Skipness, thereby giving him secure bases either side of the narrows of Kilbrannan Sound.

The MacDougalls held sway over a considerable area of this western seaboard. They had numerous residences, imposing castles of stone prominently sited upon rock outcrops. Arguably the most powerful was Dunstaffnage, strategically placed on a craggy promontory guarding the entrance to Loch Etive and affording magnificent views over a wide area. Duncan MacDougall (who had died before 1248) or his son, Ewen, built the castle – a lofty stone curtain-wall enclosing an area larger than that at Sween. The builder was obviously fully conversant with current trends in castle-planning for there are four cylindrical angle-towers projecting, albeit slightly, from the curtain, one housing a gatehouse and another, larger in scale, serving as the donjon and housing the main private apartments. There have evidently been (timber?) buildings within the courtyard set against the curtain-wall. The elaborate lancet windows in the east and north walls at first-floor level indicate apartments of some sophistication.

These castles of the Isles are, at first sight, enigmas. That such formidable fortresses were built on the fringe of a rapidly developing feudal country by men of Celtic origin, at a time when their Norman neighbours to the east were seemingly content, by and large, with castles of timber and clay, is not readily understood. But it often happens that where innovation comes late it comes with special thoroughness and force. The Celtic chiefs of the west seem to have grasped the significance of feudalism and adapted it to suit their own needs. Duncan MacDougall built not only a redoubtable castle at Dunstaffnage; he also erected a particularly fine stone chapel a short distance away; and, like a number of his Norman counterparts on the mainland, he chose to found and endow a monastery at Ardchattan, farther up Loch Etive (also now in state care). Duncan MacDougall may not have been of Norman stock, but he was no less enthusiastic a baron and vassal of the king for that.

The presence of these great stone castles should not disguise the fact that they were the exception throughout the thirteenth century, not the rule. A good many landowners, great and small, chose not to invest what must have represented a considerable proportion of their wealth in the building of such residences. The Durward earls of Atholl for example were a family of substance, and

yet, for their castle at Lumphanan, they were content with one of timber placed upon an earthen mound, in the manner of the first Anglo-Norman settlers. And the descendants of Freskin were still seemingly happy to keep faith with their timber residence upon the motte at Duffus.

The arrival of the bellicose Plantagenet, Edward I, before the walls of Berwick on 30 March 1296 brought to an abrupt and bloody end the settled years of the Kings of Peace. Strong castles of stone were no longer mere feudal showpieces; they were the very essence of survival.

Excavation in progress (1976) at the Peel Ring of Lumphanan, a thirteenth-century home (possibly a hunting lodge) of the Durward Earls of Atholl. Like the majority of lordly residences at this date it was built of timber, not stone, excepting the metalled causeway crossing the boggy ground encircling the castle mound.

The face of Edward I of England sinisterly emerges from this silver penny, minted in London about 1300 and found in 1974 among the rubble of a building on Threave Island destroyed during the Wars of Independence.

43

THE AFTERMATH OF WAR: ROBERT I TO JAMES I

". . . to build a castle or fortalice, to surround and fortify it with walls and ditches, to strengthen by iron gates and to erect on top of it all warlike apparatus necessary for its defence."
(Licence to crenellate, dated 1449)

T HE STORMING of the town of Berwick's barricades by the army of Edward I of England in 1296 heralded the most desperate, the most bloody, episode in Scotland's history, the Wars of Independence, and the indiscriminate butchery of her townsfolk was to be followed by countless other violent deeds committed by all parties to the conflict over the course of the next half-century. The return to Scotland in 1357 of King David II from a lengthy period in captivity brought a measure of stability to the country but hostility between the two nations simmered constantly thereafter and on occasion bubbled over into open conflict. Those residing in the southern part of the country close to the Border were most at risk and those to suffer the worst privation, but the murderous, internecine war reached the Highlands too. Instability and insecurity were seldom far from hand anywhere in the country.

This precarious situation is plainly seen in the castles built by the monarchy and nobility throughout Scotland from the outbreak of the Wars of Independence through to the seventeenth century. In contrast to what was happening throughout the greater part of England, where lordly residences were assuming a less fencible, more pleasing and domestic aspect, the concern of a Scottish lord was the security of himself and his household and his castle betokens a concerned, apprehensive attitude of mind.

One castle, Lochmaben on the West March, was almost certainly built by the occupying English force, work commencing on the stone castle in 1365 only after the erection of an earth-and-

timber redoubt immediately in front of it for the protection of the garrison. The edifice is now sadly wasted but sufficient survives of this courtyard castle to show that much the greatest effort had gone into creating an impregnable, landward-facing south front from which direction the greatest threat would come. The boldly projecting wing walls flanking the gatehouse and spanning the moat created a dock, or safe anchorage for boats, in a manner similar to that provided at another English-built castle, Beaumaris in North Wales. With the exception probably of the gatehouse stump at Kildrummy, Lochmaben's frail remnant is all that can reasonably be ascribed to the masons and carpenters engaged in the service of the Plantagenet kings.

Two Scotsmen only – one a Douglas, the other a Stewart – attempted to build in like manner. We cannot be sure who actually occasioned the construction of Tantallon, perched upon the rocky coastal fringe of East Lothian and, with the Bass Rock in the background, one of the most impressive sights in all Scotland, but it is with the powerful House of Douglas that the fortress is most intimately linked. Certainly William, 1st Earl of Douglas, was in possession by 1374 and the castle may well have been his inspiration. Not for him the lofty tower and its attendant barmkin. Instead he had a great curtain of stone drawn across the promontory, its almost featureless mass broken in the centre by a bulky gatehouse and each of the ends terminating in a cylindrical tower. All three towers project from the curtain-wall and the whole enclosure is enveloped by a wide, deep ditch cut through the rock. Within the enclosure along the northern edge stands a two-storeyed block,

opposite
King David II and his Scottish army before the city walls of Newcastle in 1346, towards the close of the Wars of Independence. (*Paris, Bibliothèque National MS fr 2643, fo 97v*)

Tantallon Castle, with the Bass Rock in the background. This fourteenth-century fortress-residence followed in the tradition of the great curtain-walled castles built in the preceding century. The donjon, known as the Douglas Tower after its lord, looms up at the rear of the complex with his constable's lodging over the centrally placed gatehouse. Ancillary accommodation for others in the household, and perhaps guests, was provided within the now-shattered tower in the foreground. The Douglases, modest landowners in the thirteenth century, emerged as a significant force early in the fourteenth century through their close association with the Bruce. Tantallon was most likely built by William Douglas in the third quarter of that century to herald his new found wealth and fortune.

formerly with a hall on each floor, and other ranges were evidently intended for the remaining two sides but never completed. Lean-to buildings were erected against the inside face of the curtain-wall either side of the gatehouse. The scale of the castle is impressive by any standard. The unusual design makes the functional interpretation of the various units difficult, but the proximity of the hall block to the north tower, known as the Douglas Tower, with a roomy prison at its base and a series of chambers over, suggests that here was the lord's private lodging, with his constable perhaps ensconced in the gatehouse.

Robert Stewart (c1340–1420), Earl of Fife and Menteith, 1st Duke of Albany, was certainly in a position to erect a fine castle considering the revenues, fees and pensions he enjoyed during the reigns of his father and elder brother, Robert II and Robert III. He was "a man of great expenses and munificent to strangers", according to his contemporary, Abbot Walter Bower of Inchcolm, and his castle at Doune, though uninhabited long since, still has the air of a place that has witnessed in its time "large tabling and belly cheer". Like the Earl of Douglas, Albany had the wherewithal to contemplate the building of a great courtyard castle, though as at Tantallon the full scheme was never implemented. What Albany did finish is

impressive enough. His private lodging was self-contained within a lofty tower placed at one corner of the enclosure. The sole entrance into the courtyard passed directly beneath, with the portcullis operated from within the lord's hall at first-floor level, access to which was by way of an enclosed forestair rising up from the court. A second tall tower a short distance away housed the kitchen and a further suite of chambers of some sophistication, possibly for the use of the constable or guests. Linking both towers was a splendid hall with a minstrels' gallery and a central fireplace, smoke from the fire spiralling upwards and out through a vent in the timber roof, a rare instance in a Scottish castle of such a feature. Both Tantallon and Doune are truly remarkable fortress-residences, but whereas Tantallon, with its lofty towers projecting out from the high curtain, is indebted to the castles of the "kings of peace", Doune, its rectangular towers wholly contained within the enclosure, heralds a new dawn in castle design.

When the English stronghold at Lochmaben finally fell into Scottish hands, it was chiefly through the efforts of Sir Archibald Douglas, Lord of Galloway, cousin of William, 1st Earl, and related through marriage to the Duke of Albany. He possessed extensive estates throughout the

The noble residence of Robert, Duke of Albany, at Doune Castle. On the right, his private lodging, with residential accommodation above the main entrance into the courtyard. On the left, the tower housing the kitchen and other residential quarters. The outer, or great hall is sandwiched between them. Doune is indebted to the great thirteenth-century castles for its general lay-out but the builder has broken with tradition by erecting rectangular towers in preference to the circular ones so beloved in former times (see also illustrations on pages 10 and 13).

kingdom, among them Bothwell, through his marriage to Joanna Moray, and parts of Galloway, a gift from a shrewd monarch, David II, who saw in the man qualities needed to subdue the independent-minded and frequently rebellious Gallovidians. At Bothwell, Archibald had little need to do other than adopt the shattered fabric of Walter of Moray's mighty donjon and adapt it to suit his own requirements. At Threave Island, his isolated fastness deep in Galloway, he was under no such restraint and he built there so tall and forbidding a castle that those who gazed upon it can have been left in no doubt as to the intentions of its lord within. Archibald's nickname "The Grim", earned it is said on account of his terrible countenance in warfare, might equally be applied to his castle.

Archibald Douglas built what has come to be called a **tower-house**, a class of structure whose

The gaunt, forbidding ruin of Threave Castle from across the eastern channel of the River Dee. The present solitary appearance of Archibald "The Grim's" tower-house gives a very misleading picture of the scene about 1400, when numerous imposing buildings and lesser structures were clustered around it. All was swept away about 1447 as the 8th Earl of Douglas took measures to strengthen his defences against imminent attack. The tower-house alone remained, protected by a solid artillery fortification which was to successfully withstand two fully pressed sieges. (*Reproduced by kind permission of the Royal Museum of Scotland*)

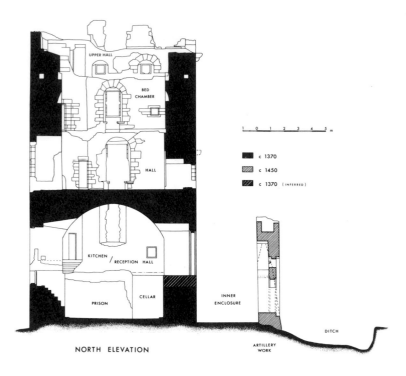

UPPER HALL

BED
CHAMBER

HALL

```
┌─┬─┬─┬─┬─┬─┬─┐
1  0  1  2  3  4  5  m
```

■ c 1370

▨ c 1450

▨ c 1370 [INFERRED]

KITCHEN / RECEPTION HALL

PRISON   CELLAR

INNER
ENCLOSURE

DITCH

NORTH ELEVATION

ARTILLERY
WORK

Section through the tower-house and artillery fortification at Threave Castle. The arrangement of the lord's accommodation assumed a pattern identical to that in the donjons of the great thirteenth-century castles, with ancillary service quarters in the basement, hall and residential rooms above. The topmost floor was intended as temporary quarters for the garrison in time of siege (see illustration on page 39), the main defence being conducted from the wall-head. The numerous openings at this level gave the defenders access to their projecting timber hoarding (see illustrations on pages 22 and 25).

origins may be found in the earlier Norman keeps and which came to be adopted generally throughout much of Europe. The Scots, more than most, took this simple, inexpensive but most effective castle form to their hearts and exercised considerable ingenuity and artistry in its planning and appearance throughout the later Middle Ages. Indeed, it became so ingrained in their minds that its dour and lofty form was adhered to by many lairds long after there was any real necessity to do so. The tower-house provided all the basic accommodation, albeit in a somewhat cramped, top-heavy kind of way, whilst providing a secure, but simple, defence. It may have been a "closed-up, inward-looking building" but it was ideally suited to those troubled times.

Threave was among the first tower-houses built, about 1370, and helped establish this new fashion in baronial architecture. Its five storeys, one atop the other and linked by a single spiral stair acting in effect like a vertical corridor, comprised in ascending order: cellarage, kitchen, hall, chambers and upper hall. The castle's defence was economically achieved, largely through the provision of thick walls sparsely punctured by windows which are in most cases mere slits and only more generously sized on the less vulnerable sides facing onto the river and marshes. The one entrance doorway, at first-floor level leading directly into the kitchen, was reached by a

movable timber stair or ladder which could be hauled up out of reach in the event of a siege. The main defence was intended to be conducted from the wall-head, where the vestiges of a box-machicolation over the doorway and evidence for a temporary timber hoard around the other three sides are still visible. In this way Archibald Douglas provided for his household's welfare and safety whilst in Galloway. The upstanding masonry on the island, however, gives a misleading impression of its former appearance. Beneath the grass are the foundations of numerous ancillary structures which combined to make up the castle complex. Two very substantial buildings in particular stood close beside the main tower and in all probability served as hall and lodgings for retainers and guests of "The Grim", who passed away within its wall on Christmas Eve, 1400.

Ten years earlier, Robert II, the first Stewart monarch and father of the 1st Duke of Albany, had died within his castle at Dundonald. This humble, affable and somewhat reluctant king preferred the comparative isolation of his own baronial estates in Ayrshire to the busier centres of power. He had inherited a great courtyard castle at Dundonald which we can only assume must have suffered severely in the Wars, for Robert Stewart set about transforming it into a mighty tower-house on the scale of Threave. Its present gaunt and ghostly mass is misleading for it has been a most majestic building, with coats-of-arms emblazoned on its walls and a handsome vaulted main hall on the topmost storey; truly a residence befitting a nobleman elevated to kingship.

Both Archibald Douglas and Robert Stewart may have been influenced by what they saw rising from the eastern summit of Edinburgh's Castle Rock, for immediately upon his return from captivity David II gave orders for the building of a new castle to replace that damaged or destroyed in the Wars. Ruins from that castle, now known as David's Tower, lie entombed within the later Half Moon Battery and though the greater part of it was destroyed by artillery bombardment during the Long Siege of 1573 enough survives to indicate a great, solid tower-house, not unlike Threave and Dundonald, but with observable differences, particularly in the provision of a wing, or jamb, applied to one corner, thereby producing an L-shaped ground-plan. The use of smaller wings applied to the main block, seen for the first time at David's Tower, came to be widely adopted as builders exercised considerable invention in the disposition of the various apartments required by the lord in his tower-house.

left
The ruined and roofless lord's hall at Dundonald Castle. The wasted remains of the great fireplace (centre left) and the stone vault now scarcely do justice to what must have formerly been a majestic apartment (inset: the hall restored).

Noblemen of the second rank were not long in following the lead shown by their superiors, though the paucity of tower-houses dating from this time suggests that very few could afford the considerable expense that such building work entailed. Amongst their number were kinsmen of The Douglas, at Lochleven and Aberdour, a kinsman of The Bruce at Clackmannan and a Mure at Rowallan. The tower-house on the island of Lochleven could in fact predate David's Tower and may indeed have been the castle in which Robert the Stewart himself was held captive for a short while just two years before his coronation. Two centuries later, Lochleven was to serve as prison for a more famous Stewart monarch, Mary Queen of Scots. Lochleven is remarkable for having its main entrance doorway on the third storey 5 m above the ground and entering directly into the hall. It has a well-preserved courtyard wall, by no means as substantial as the great curtains at Doune, Tantallon and the imposing thirteenth-century castles, but solid enough considering the island's isolated situation. These stoutly enclosed courtyards attached to tower-houses were called barmkins (literally "a barrier for kine (cattle)"), for during a siege livestock were brought inside for their protection and as an emergency source of food.

below
Lochleven Castle, among the earliest tower-houses built after the Wars of Independence and displaying well their characteristically "closed-up, inward-looking" appearance. Note the entrance doorway situated at an upper level, reached by a ladder or stair that could be drawn up in times of danger (the doorway and steps near the base were introduced later).

"Waste not; want not." A man warms himself by his fireside, whilst his dinner cooks in a cauldron over the flames – a detail from one of a series of English stained glass roundels, late fifteenth century, in the Burrell Collection. (*Reproduced by kind permission of Glasgow Museums and Art Galleries*)

Morton Castle. The line of small, square openings in the main block light the undercroft at ground level whilst the grander windows above light the lord's hall and chamber. The projecting portion on the left is part of a once well-protected gatehouse.

It is not unusual for these early towers to lack a kitchen within their walls and such is the case even in sixteenth-century towers like Edzell and Carsluith. At Crichton, built by John de Crichton about 1400, a poky little cooking stance squeezed into the entresol, or intermediate storey, above the pit prison served as the kitchen for a number of years. The absence of a kitchen within the tower may have been occasioned by the need to reduce the risk of fire, coupled with a desire to cut down on the noise and smells issuing therefrom, but their presence within the towers at Threave and Dundonald makes this an unlikely explanation. Rather, we must see their absence resulting from a

lack of space brought about by limited financial resources and it is likely that, in the smaller towers, a certain amount of cooking was done over the hall or chamber fire. Two lords made a special effort to overcome the inconvenience by using the greater flexibility afforded by the applied wing. Sir Simon Preston at Craigmillar may have been influenced by David's Tower just 5 km away and his adroit use of the jamb gave him a sufficiency of space to provide not only a kitchen adjacent to his main hall but also a private chamber immediately overhead. Neither the risk of fire nor those of noise and smell would seem to have worried Sir Simon unduly. At Crookston, the grand residence of Sir John Stewart of Darnley when he was not in France fighting for Joan d'Arc against the English, the use of wings was taken to the extreme. Four in all were applied, one to each corner of the main block, housing kitchen and other domestic and storage accommodation on the lower levels with private chambers over.

A handful of noblemen chose to build differently, imitating neither the great courtyard-castles nor the lofty tower-houses of their contemporaries. The castle at Morton, perched impressively on a promontory amid the rolling Nithsdale hills, was more closely akin to the fortified manors being built in England and has been called a **hall-house**. Just like the first castles at Skipness and Lochranza, it was a more compact, marginally less forbidding fortified dwelling than a tower-house, built with a timber-roofed hall set over an undercroft housing domestic and storage accommodation. Private chambers were provided in towers applied to the main hall block, whose fenestration was altogether more generous and domestic in appearance. Defence has not been neglected; far from it. The now largely collapsed gatehouse could have been modelled on that at nearby Caerlaverock, with two cylindrical towers flanking a heavily protected entrance passage. We cannot with confidence now say who built it, nor when. But a kinsman of Douglas and a date in the late fourteenth century seems likely.

Morton may have derived its form from the fortified manors of northern England; the first stone castle at Hermitage, in deepest Liddesdale, was actually built by an Englishman, Lord Dacre, who held the stronghold for his king, Edward III of England, between 1358 and 1365 or thereabouts. Like his sovereign at Lochmaben, Lord Dacre built a stone castle, presumably to replace the earth-and-timber one destroyed in the Wars. It took the form of a fortified manor with two two-storeyed blocks flanking a small open courtyard with screen walls along the remaining two sides, one housing

the entrance and the other a spiral stair leading to the lord's hall and chambers on the upper storeys of the side blocks. The ground floors comprised domestic and storage undercrofts. When William, 1st Earl of Douglas, regained possession a little before 1371 he set about converting this insubstantial manor-house into a formidable fortress. He chose not the courtyard form of Tantallon but the lofty tower-house plan adopted by his cousin, Archibald, at Threave. Initially just one small jamb was applied to the main block, containing the first-floor entrance doorway. By degrees other wings were added, producing an ensemble of unusual complexity and interest. Halls, chambers, a chapel, prison and assorted service offices were all confined within this bleak, bulky pile and it still appears today what it was known as then, "the Strength of Liddesdale".

If the Wars with England had left little standing at Hermitage, other castles had come through the ordeal relatively unscathed and their owners began to effect repairs, taking the opportunity of altering and extending their accommodation to suit their own particular needs. John Halyburton came into possession of Dirleton through marriage before 1350. He found De Vaux's once-proud castle sadly battered. The donjon complex was largely intact but much of the curtain-wall had collapsed, or been purposefully dismantled by Robert Bruce's adherents carrying out his "scorched-earth" tactics by rendering castles incapable of being retaken and held by the English. Halyburton no doubt found the Anglo-Norman's old lodging cramped and ill-suited and he initiated a fresh building programme which was in time to lead to the creation of an entirely new range of lodgings, including an impressive gatehouse and a suite containing kitchen, hall and chamber built over a spacious vaulted undercroft. Lord Maxwell at Caerlaverock, the scene of Edward I's best-documented siege, was faced with an equally major job of repair, though he seems to have kept faith with the original lay-out possibly on account of the limitations imposed by a constricted site. Even the castles of senior clerics were not exempt. The episcopal castle at St Andrews had no sooner been damaged and repaired by the English in the 1330s when orders were issued to Andrew Moray, Warden of Scotland, to "ding it doun". This he evidently did, for much of the present castle can be ascribed to the time of Walter Traill's episcopacy (1385–1401) who, according to a contemporary, died in the castle "which he himself had erected from its foundations".

The courtyard of Lord Dacre's castle at Hermitage, originally open to the elements and flanked on left and right by storage undercrofts at ground level with hall and chambers over, reached by the spiral staircase visible through the far door. This fortified manor was, by degrees, transformed into a mighty tower-house by the Douglases (see illustration on page 4).

CASTLE AND CANNON: JAMES II – MARY

*"(The King) causit maissonnis cum and rainforce samin
wallis quhilk was left waist of befoir . . . and maid all massie
work . . . that it sould be unwinabill in tymes comming to
ony enemies that would come to persew it."*
(Lindsay of Pitscottie's *Historie*, on measures taken by
James V to strengthen the defences of Tantallon Castle
after its capture in 1529)

THE OVERTHROW of the powerful House of Douglas by King James II in 1455 had a significance for Scotland's legacy of castles for two reasons. First, it marked a major redistribution of lands and not just those formerly held by Black Douglas. Secondly, the siege of Threave, where the final scene in the drama was enacted, heralded a new and more menacing era of warfare, for numbered among the king's armament was his *magnus bombardus*, "great bombard", a massive iron gun capable of firing large balls of iron and stone great distances. As a consequence, those who now found themselves possessed with the wherewithal to build new castles, or found themselves owners of properties which they wished either to alter or extend, had to do so in the knowledge that the power of gunpowder further threatened their security.

The last Earl of Douglas, no less bellicose than the monarch he sought to usurp, had already appreciated the venom that could be spat out of the mouths of these crude but terrifying new weapons. He was known to be refortifying several of his castles and at Threave the artillery wall he wrapped around the lower storeys of his grandfather's tower-house still survives well-nigh intact, despite having endured two prolonged sieges, the last in 1640. The low artillery work, sloped externally so as to cushion more effectively the impact of the new siege-pieces, was evidently designed to be defended by a garrison equipped both with conventional long- and cross-bows as well as with the more murderous new invention, the gun, protruding through the vertical "key-hole" and "dumb-bell" loops in the towers. Only towards the close of the sixteenth century was the

gun to achieve an absolute supremacy over its more ancient rivals.

The new, large cannon was not only unpredictable, as James II found to his cost at the siege of Roxburgh in 1460 when he was "unhappely . . . slane with ane gune, the quhilk brak in fyring"; they were also enormously expensive and beyond the means of almost all bar monarchy. The mighty quadrangular, angle-towered curtain at Craigmillar Castle, the property of the Prestons but much frequented by the Stewart kings and queens, is traditionally dated to the year 1427 and, unlike that at Threave, which was constructed in great haste in response to a particular threat, is undoubtedly an integral feature of a carefully planned extension around the original tower-house to provide more commodious and sophisticated domestic and service accommodation. Here too the new gun-pieces, placed on trestles within the drum towers, served alongside the more traditional weapons, fired from the wall-head, windows and other openings. Neither at Threave nor at Craigmillar was the older tower-house altered to make provision for the new armament.

The first castle to be newly built taking fully into account the potential of cannon-power was Ravenscraig, perched upon a narrow promontory whose sheer sides plunge headlong into the chill waters of the Forth. It was begun in 1460 on the orders of James II shortly before he died, and continued in 1463 by his widowed queen, Mary of Gueldres, shortly before she too passed away. The castle, as we view it today, is clearly not all of one constructional period; the horizontal wide-

Mons Meg, in Edinburgh Castle. Made in 1449 and used at Crookston and Dumbarton Castles in 1489.

opposite
An attack on a castle, showing the use of incendiary arrows and cannon, from a German *Firework Book*, printed at about the time the 8th Earl of Douglas was fortifying his tower-house at Threave with an artillery defence – see illustrations on pages 25 and 47. (*Reproduced by kind permission of the Royal Armouries*)

The fifteenth-century gatehouse at Newark, with part of Lord Maxwell's tower-house behind. Note the "dumb-bell" gun-loop on the left, one of three placed so as to cover the three external faces of the gatehouse. The "cover" was minimal, the guns themselves unwieldy and temperamental. The gun-loops at this early date owe a debt to the arrow-slits of earlier days and we may reasonably surmise that the old firepower, particularly the cross-bow, still had the edge in terms both of efficiency and effectiveness.

mouthed gun-ports atop the frontal cross wall were most likely added by one of the Sinclair Earls of Caithness who had received the castle from James III in 1470 in exchange for the earldom of Orkney and who were no strangers to the new weapon, having been closely involved in the management of the royal artillery train. The original planning, however, shows how fully the potential of artillery had been realised both in the defence of and in the assault on a castle.

Few of the king's subjects followed the example of Ravenscraig. Most notable families engaged in the building of new stone castles, like the Balfours at Burleigh, close to Loch Leven and the Maxwell's at Newark on the Clyde, kept faith with the now-established tower-house with its attendant barmkin or courtyard. Where an appreciation of the potential of gunpowder is displayed, it appears not as an integral part of the overall planning but rather in the somewhat haphazard provision of "key-hole" gun-loops and their early sixteenth-century successors, horizontal wide-mouthed gun-holes, normally restricted to the lower storey.

That belligerent Gallovidian family, the McCullochs, who had fared rather well through the demise of Black Douglas, incorporated four gun-loops into their new and imposing tower-house overlooking the Solway at Cardoness, and the Ruthvens did similarly at Huntingtower. When the Pringles came to build their somewhat small and compact tower and barmkin on their estate at Smailholm, close to the Border with England, a single "key-hole" gun-loop cunningly sited right above the one doorway into the keep was considered sufficient for their needs.

One exception was Noltland Castle, the island retreat of Gilbert Balfour, a younger son of Balfour of Mountquhannie, in Fife, and a vigorous supporter of Queen Mary. Balfour was a man possessed of few scruples; John Knox, who had shared an oar with him on a French galley during their captivity between 1547 and 1549, called him a man "without god", and contemporary accounts of the individual certainly depict no peaceable, God-fearing fellow. Seen in this light, it is not perhaps surprising that his Orcadian fastness has so stern and martial an aspect. There are no less than seventy-one yawning gun-holes arranged in tiers throughout the outer walls giving the building the appearance of "some antique man-of-war's hull".

With the successful reassertion of the authority of the monarchy by James I and his successors, castles became increasingly to appear more like residences and less like fortresses. Security was still an important consideration, of course, and would remain so until the country became more stable and peaceful; but, more and more, the nobility strove to improve the comfort and amenity of their castles.

In general, the tower-houses built in the late fifteenth century conformed to the standard rectangular plan but display signs of becoming more flexible in their arrangement. The use of entrance-doorways awkwardly sited above the ground was now largely abandoned, though at Castle Campbell, the magnificently situated Lowland residence of Colin, Lord Campbell, who was created Earl of Argyll in either 1457 or 1458, there is evidence for a first-floor entrance in addition to the one at ground level. This seems also to have been the case at another Campbell residence, Kilchurn, dramatically set amid the steel-grey waters of Loch Awe, and at the largest of all Scotland's tower-houses, Spynie, begun during the episcopacy of David Stewart (1461–76), Bishop of Moray, and completed by Bishop William Tulloch, his successor.

An inscription, now illegible, here at Noltland Castle read: "When I see the blood I will pass over you in the night." The tiers of gun-loops piercing the castle walls, some seventy-one in number, echo this blood-curdling pronouncement and Gilbert Balfour's lavish provision far exceeds that in any other Scottish castle.

Castle Gloom, now Castle Campbell, set in a magnificent position on the Ochil Hills high above the valley of the Forth. The first building, the tower-house (in the foreground) built for Colin, Lord Campbell in the mid fifteenth century, is typical of the cramped and ill-lit residences of the period: not so the structures beyond, added by succeeding lairds to complement, perhaps even to supercede the old tower.

Rosyth Castle, sketched by James Grose in 1789. The slightly projecting jamb, or wing, incorporated the spiral staircase, a sort of vertical corridor linking the various levels. With the stair largely removed from the main block, the apartments on each storey were enabled to take on a more expansive form.

Balvaird Castle, a tower-house of no little sophistication for its day (fifteenth century). The L-shaped plan gave the builder greater flexibility in the form and arrangement of the various rooms (with the lord's hall and chamber in the main block, on the right, and the kitchen and ancillary chambers in the jamb on the left). The complete removal of the spiral staircase to its own block sited within the re-entrant angle of the L-plan further improved the size and disposition of the main accommodation.

We now begin to see the jamb, or wing, increasingly used by master-masons constantly striving to improve both the number, size and inter-relationship of the various domestic and service offices. The Lindsays at Edzell and the Stewarts at Rosyth, for example, were given towers on the L-plan which, like Craigmillar before them, enabled the vertical stair to be removed from the main block. The home of the Murrays at Balvaird, at the head of Glen Farg, was one of the most sophisticated tower-houses of its day. Designed on the variant of the L-plan, with the spiral stair carried upward in a turret projecting from within the re-entrant angle, it has incorporated within its shell the main domestic and service accommodation, including a kitchen on the ground floor, all comfortably sized and conveniently located. The sophistication of its planning extends even to the manner in which the privies have been cleverly positioned one above the other so that all the soil collected in one chamber on the ground floor and could be removed by pulling out a movable stone, the "grund-wa'-stane", at the ground level outside. To improve the cleanliness of the privies, an ingenious arrangement of stone spouts on the roof carried rain-water into the garderobe chutes – the precursor of the flushed toilet.

This growing ingenuity in the planning of tower-houses is further reflected in the improving quality and sophistication of the architectural and other detail. The architect responsible for Balvaird's astutely arranged accommodation also had a tasteful eye for fine detail, as can be seen on his hall fireplace. The McCullochs of Cardoness were not amongst the most mannerly of folk but this social failing did not prevent their showing

The fine painted wooden ceiling in the original lord's hall at Huntingtower Castle, probably the oldest surviving tempera-painted ceiling in existence in any Scottish residence.

Orchardton Tower, unique in being the only circular tower-house built in Scotland in the later Middle Ages.

exceptionally good taste when it came to interior design. Their hall and chamber fireplaces, with their aumbries, are particularly fine specimens. The Ruthvens at Huntingtower lavishly decorated their plastered walls and timber ceilings with ornate, colourful and imaginative paintings, carried out about 1540 and probably the earliest now in existence in any Scottish dwelling. Such lavish surface treatments were clearly more common than might be suggested by the few surviving examples. At Kinneil, the house of Governor Arran, the predominantly scriptural scenes painted on the walls of his palace about 1554 were covered with more stylised decoration in the following century. None would be there to be enjoyed today were it not for an observant workman engaged upon the demolition of the house in 1936.

Noblemen both great and small dug deep into their purses to improve the quality of their surroundings. John Cairns, laird of Orchardton on the rocky Stewartry coast, was a man of modest means and his fifteenth-century circular tower-house – a shape unique in Scotland – has more the appearance of a windmill without its sails than a lordly castle. And yet the finely-carved aumbry in his tiny round hall is testimony to his good taste. Thomas Cochrane, on the other hand, Earl of Mar, and a favourite of James III, could afford an imposing tower-house on his northern estate at

Auchindoun, a bleak and wind-swept hill in remote Glen Fiddich. What a gladdening sight that main hall must have been on a cold winter's night, with its grand fireplace and finely detailed ribbed vault.

The ingenuity of the architect-mason enabled those who were building in stone for the first time to erect quite commodious and comfortable tower houses. But men like William, 1st Lord Crichton and Chancellor of Scotland, had inherited towers raised in more insecure and economically straitened times. Crichton was a man of importance in the affairs of state during the minority of James II who could not possibly reside, far less entertain, within the cramped and gloomy tower-house built by his father on an exposed hillside above the Tyne in Midlothian. Faced with this dilemma, Chancellor Crichton effectively abandoned the old tower and relocated his principal apartments in a new, three-storeyed

block adjacent. At ground level he provided an imposing entrance-doorway and vaulted trance flanked by cellars, not unlike Albany's at Doune; directly overhead he placed his hall, formerly a handsome well-lighted chamber, with a large hooded fireplace at the dais end and, at the other, a pantry and buttery screened by stone, not wood. On the top floor has been another splendid room, his lordship's more intimate great chamber.

The Bruces of Clackmannan solved the problem somewhat differently. In preference to erecting an entirely separate residential block, they simply expanded the original tower-house by building on a generously sized wing that rose one storey higher and substantially improved and extended the accommodation. The chambers in the first tower were retained with only minor modifications, but the addition of the wing gave the architect greater flexibility in the disposition of the various elements required by a family seeking greater comfort and privacy. The kitchen, formerly outside the tower, was now brought directly alongside the hall, whilst more intimate chambers were provided in the upper storeys of the wing.

The reassertion of the authority of monarchy and the improvement in the Crown revenues at this time are well reflected in an increasingly vigorous building activity at the principal royal seats – Dunfermline, Edinburgh, Falkland (not in state care), Holyroodhouse, Linlithgow and Stirling. Whatever may have been on the rocky summit at Stirling or beside the pleasing loch at Linlithgow at an earlier age, it cannot surely have rivalled the spacious, well-planned and exquisitely detailed structures that were now being erected under the patronage of the later Stewart kings and their consorts. James I had taken the initiative in 1425 with a comprehensive rebuilding programme of the old royal manor at Linlithgow that had recently been burnt to the ground. From the ashes arose a "very fair palace", according to James V's queen the most princely home she had ever looked upon. The Great Hall, called the Lion Chamber, and much of the east range, including the splendid original entry, date from the 1430s and are truly regal though the palace did not attain its present, cloistered quadrangular plan until the reigns of James IV and V. These two monarchs were largely instrumental in transforming the royal castles of Edinburgh and Stirling into the majestic palaces that we enjoy today.

Little but James IV's elaborate open-timber, hammer-beamed roof over the Great Hall has survived intact at Edinburgh. Stirling on the other

The elaborate open-timber roof within King James IV's Great Hall at Edinburgh Castle, with its finely detailed supporting framework cantilevered out from the wall-head on hammer-beams. The wall posts are carried on corbels (projecting brackets), richly carved with Classical motifs showing a remarkably early instance of the use of Renaissance decorative art.

hand is unusually complete, despite the uncaring attentions of subsequent generations of occupants. As we pass through the great forework of James IV, with its bold drum towers punctured by "dumb-bell" gun-loops, and explore the various royal apartments, the magnificent Great Hall, justly described by Defoe as the "noblest I ever saw in Europe", the sumptuous palace, the intriguing King's Old Building and the Chapel Royal, we cannot but agree with the poet, Taylor, who visiting in 1618 considered the whole complex "all very stately and befitting the majesty of a king". There can be no doubt that both James IV and James V were greatly influenced by the experiences and aspirations of their foreign queens, Margaret Tudor, the sister of King Henry VIII of England, and Mary of Guise, the daughter of Claude of Guise-Lorraine, Duc D'Aumale in France. The south range of Linlithgow Palace is clearly influenced by English Perpendicular, whilst the Palace at Stirling, both in its planning and its sumptuous ornamentation, reveals the best of the French Renaissance. If Linlithgow is the

finest example of domestic planning in late medieval Scotland, Stirling is the most elegant and graceful.

Though many contemporary Scots noblemen were undeniably impressed by what they saw when they came to the parliaments held in the Great Halls at Edinburgh, Linlithgow and Stirling, few were persuaded or indeed perhaps able to follow suit. One structure alone, the somewhat inscrutable King's Old Building at Stirling, would seem to have inspired imitations, for its arrangement of well-appointed hall and chamber raised above a vaulted basement, with private chambers on the top storey, all reached by a projecting fore-stair, can be discerned elsewhere. Castle Campbell, the Lowland seat of the Earls of Argyll, was but a few miles from the castle at Stirling and the first move to improve upon the tower-house accom-modation, implemented perhaps by Colin, the 3rd Earl, about 1520, was to build a structure closely comparable to that at Stirling from which it clearly derives. At about the same time, Mungo Mure,

The courtyard at Linlithgow Palace. On the left is the original entry to King James I's palace, with niches above once housing representations of the Thrie Estates; on the right the new entry added during King James V's reign. The fountain (restored in the 1930s) is also of James V's time but the regular, vertical fenestration of the south front, which recalls English Perpendicular architecture, dates from the time of King James IV, whose queen was Margaret Tudor, daughter of King Henry VII of England.

Sketch by John Knight of King James IV's Great Hall within Stirling Castle, as it will appear once the present work of consolidation and repair is completed. This quite stupendous space was created to house the great occasions of state and ceremony that were part and parcel of kingship as practised by the Stewart monarchs. At the far, upper end, is the dais, or raised platform where the king sat in his majesty bathed in sunlight streaming through the capacious window.

The remarkable Renaissance south façade of King James V's palace at Stirling Castle emerges from behind the embattled curtain-wall built by his father, James IV. This palace is of outstanding importance not only on account of its richly Classical exterior, amongst the earliest attempts in Britain, but also for the sophisticated internal planning of the royal apartments.

A conjectural reconstruction by Tom Borthwick of Craignethan Castle as built in the 1530s for Sir James Hamilton of Finnart, "that bluddie bouchour", and James V's Master of Works.

Lord Rowallan, who like Campbell had fallen heir to a cramped and constricted tower-house, did precisely the same, and there is good reason to believe, from what is left to us amidst the ruins of Huntly, that an Earl of Huntly was similarly motivated.

There was one family who, by degrees, had come to possess both the wealth, the knowledge and the ability to build on the grand scale, the Hamiltons. Sir James Hamilton of Finnart, a natural son of James Hamilton, 1st Earl of Arran, having spent his early years abroad, amassing more than a passing knowledge of architecture and fortification, returned to Scotland where he struck up a close friendship with his kinsman, James V, rising to become his master of works. On the death of his father in 1529 James was appointed sole executor of his father's will and guardian of the infant 2nd Earl, and it may have been his elevation to the heights of political influence that prompted this cultured, bigoted and ruthless individual to embark upon the creation of some quite remarkable fortress-residences, in particular Kinneil and Craignethan.

Craignethan, in a striking and inaccessible situation high above the Water of Nethan, was the last private castle of high defensive capability built in Scotland. As a fortress it relied heavily upon the great artillery wall and ditch protecting its most vulnerable western side. It invites comparison with what James V himself was building in the way of artillery defences at Blackness and Tantallon Castles, and with the defensive works associated with Archbishop Beaton at St Andrews – that is, massively thick walls punctured by huge, yawning, horizontal gun-holes. As a residence, Craignethan, though built as a tower-house, did not slavishly follow the top-heavy towers that preceded it or were indeed to follow after. Rather, this squat masonry structure approximates more to "a spacious but brilliantly compact dwelling-house", for in preference to piling one room upon another the builder has contrived to achieve a quite ingenious split-level arrangement more reminiscent of the country houses of a later age.

Though Craignethan's tower-house presaged what was to come, its own history as a fortress-residence was so remarkably brutal and short that the place was effectively abandoned before the century was through. The execution of Hamilton of Finnart in 1540 may have removed one particularly ambitious and ruthless individual from the political scene, but he had kinsmen equally intent upon their own advancement. But their staunch espousal of the cause of Queen Mary proved their downfall and in 1579 the great artillery work of James Hamilton was cast down into the waters of the Nethan far below. The last of the great medieval fortress-residences to be erected on Scotland's soil had been laid low.

KING JAMES VI'S PEACE

"This I must say for Scotland, here I sit and govern it with my pen: I write and it is done, and by a Clerk of the Council I govern Scotland now, which others could not do by the sword."
(James VI of Scotland and I of England)

THE STRUGGLE between Queen Mary's men and those supporting her young son, King James VI, in which noblemen like the Hamiltons, experienced fluctuating fortunes, was effectively ended by 1573. Thereafter the odd quarrel erupted into open, bloody conflict but by the time King James formally assumed the direct government of his people, on the occasion of his 21st birthday in June 1587, Scotland was once more a country at peace, both with herself and with her neighbours, particularly England. It was a "time of repose which God has granted us after our long troubles" and by 1622 the Privy Council was pleased to remark on "this dilectible tyme of peax under your majesteis regne and most excellent government".

Given the two hundred and fifty years of discord and strife that had preceded King James' reign, it is small wonder that the Scots nobility and gentry were slow in discarding the fortress-like appearance that had come to be the hallmark of their residences. The emergence of a far stronger central government, helped considerably by the power and authority of a single-minded but considerate monarch, was fast clearing away the medieval cobwebs, but old habits died hard and, despite the growing appetite among the landed class for increased comfort and privacy, there was nonetheless a cautious reserve bred of a continued feeling of insecurity. Gone were the days when great private fortress-residences would either be tolerated or necessary; there were to be no more Craignethans. Castles built from the reign of James VI on were residences first and foremost, fortresses a poor second. Their walls and roofs were no longer designed to resist the fully pressed assault but merely to ward off undesirable adversaries and uninvited intruders.

This circumspect welcome by the aristocracy of the new-found peace is marked by the reluctance of some to break out from the great stone shells built in an earlier age. The mighty Bothwell Castle still served as noble residence to the Countess of Angus until its final abandonment at the close of the seventeenth century. Lord Ruthven likewise felt constrained to remain upon the craggy knoll at his seat at Dirleton, a place of strength that had served his predecessors well since the early days of feudalism. Not content with the ancient buildings, he raised a new lodging in the early classic Renaissance style having more the appearance of a domestic residence than a lordly castle and of which one guest remarked that it was "the pleasantest dwelling in Scotland".

There were undoubtedly other claimants for this accolade. Francis Stewart, Earl of Bothwell and a kinsman of James VI, was "a cultured Renaissance ruffian" whose frequent exiles abroad, particularly in Italy and Spain, had brought to his notice the tasteful architecture of the Continental Renaissance. At his castle of Crichton, last remodelled more than a century before, he incorporated between 1581 and 1591 a most elegant and well-planned new range whose diamond-faceted façade recalls several south European noble palaces. George Gordon, Earl of Huntly, was similarly exiled, though in France. He too was taken with what he had witnessed abroad and upon his return in 1596 and to mark his elevation to the marquisate of Huntly he admirably contrived to embellish the main elevations and state rooms of his palace. The splendid suite of oriels with its inscribed frieze that emblazons the south front; the elaborate mantlepieces in the marchioness's lodging on the second floor; the great "frontispiece" above the

The doorway and "frontispiece" at the first marquis's palace at Huntly Castle. A devout Roman Catholic, George Gordon considered the arrangement of this heraldic doorway most carefully, for as the eye ascends we pass the coats of arms of this nobleman and his lady, through the achievements of his sole earthly overlord, King James VI, and his queen, Anne of Denmark, to a depiction of the Passion and Resurrection of Christ, surmounted by the figure of St Michael triumphing over Satan. These sacred subjects were irrevocably defaced by one of the Covenanting army occupying the castle in 1640.

main doorway with its intricately contrived symbolism and heraldry, justly described as "the most splendid heraldic doorway in the British Isles" – these are all fine achievements and suitably reflect the cultured and enlightened spirit during the time of King James' peace. Both rank alongside the "dainty fabrick" of the Earl of Nithsdale's new mansion erected in the 1630s within the decaying curtain-wall at Caerlaverock as architecture and craftsmanship of the first order.

The continuing need to lurk behind the defences of old is evident throughout the land. In the far west the Campbell Earl of Argyll was not disposed to break out from the confines of his castles at Dunstaffnage or Skipness, preferring instead to remodel his residential quarters behind the comparative safety of the existing curtain-wall. At both castles the new building took the form of a lofty tower-house such as had previously been provided by that family at Castle Campbell, and by a kinsman at Kilchurn. In view of the close involvement of successive Earls of Argyll in the

The remarkable Italianate façade of Francis Stewart's new range added to Crichton Castle in the 1580s, undoubtedly inspired by what he had witnessed during his frequent exiles abroad in southern Italy and Spain. Note the double tier of projecting stone corbels up and to the left of the range, formerly supporting a wooden balcony overlooking the courtyard. Right: the Palazzo Steripinto, built in 1501 in Sciacca, Sicily, and a possible source of inspiration.

political and religious turmoils of the seventeenth century it was perhaps just as well that they remained securely housed.

In the north, at Balvenie, John Stewart, 4th Earl of Atholl (1542–79), was likewise reluctant to leave the great defensive shield first built by a Comyn three hundred years before. Nevertheless, he was marginally more bold in that he placed his new lodging over one side of the ancient enceinte in preference to remaining wholly within it. And for his new residence Atholl chose not the fashionable tower-house, with room piled upon room, but instead selected to build on the **palace-plan**, that is with a sequence of rooms placed horizontally, as at the royal palaces. At the principal first-floor level the arrangement of hall, outer chamber and inner chamber, with privy and study off, can clearly be followed and this altogether less cumbersome, more comfortable, arrangement came to be used more and more.

King James's reign witnessed a prolific tower-house boom, and a representative selection are in state care; like Carsluith, built for the Browns in the 1560s, Claypotts and MacLellans in the 1570s, Greenknowe, dated 1581, Glenbuchat, completed in 1590, and Castle of Park, finished a year later. They assume all manner of shape and size, each reflecting the wealth and rank of its noble builder. Some are positively diminutive, like Knock whose simple rectangle measures no more than 8 m by 6 m; others are grand by comparison. The central block at Elcho alone reached 20 m in length and 9 m in breadth. There are uncomplicated rectangular towers such as that built by a Gordon within the old curtain-wall at Urquhart. Many more are straightforward versions on the L-plan (eg Drumcoltran and Scotstarvit) where the spiral stair has been placed within the projection, freeing the main block for the lord's accommodation. A number are more ingenious variations still. The tower-house built by John Strachan at Claypotts in the 1570s is built on what has come to be called the Z-plan, for towers, in this case circular in plan, have been applied to the central block at two of the diagonally opposite corners. A more conventional Z-plan house incorporating rectangular towers at opposing corners can be seen at Glenbuchat, the residence of John Gordon, whose wife, Helen Carnegie, was brought up not far from the Angus estate of John Strachan. A small number of towers, including Elcho and MacLellans, are most unusual variants of the L-plan. And the greater the variety, the more flexible and comfortable the arrangement. Compare the five private rooms within Thomas

Greenknowe Tower, completed in 1581 as a residence for James Seton and Janet Edmonstone, his wife. The contrast with its near neighbour, Smailholm Tower (left), built a century earlier, is striking for though both are tower-houses they are quite different homes. Smailholm is a cramped and ill-lit building, "closed up and inward looking"; Greenknowe has an altogether more open, more welcoming aspect, with generous windows, pleasing flushes of architectural embellishment and, within, numerous, good-sized rooms. There is the odd gun-loop, but they are tactically inept, designed to ward off undesirables but not the fully pressed siege.

above

Claypotts. Here the builder has experimented with the possibilities presented by the addition of the jamb, or wing, to the central block, and achieved a most novel and imaginative building on the Z-plan. The wings are circular in plan only insofar as their external appearance goes, for internally all the rooms are of conventional rectangular shape. But the manner in which the circular jambs articulate with their fully rectangular garret storeys gives Claypotts that special charm for which it is rightly renowned.

below

Glenbuchat Castle, a Z-plan tower-house incorporating rectangular jambs, applied to the central block. Note the projecting bartizans, or corbelled corner turrets, at the wall-head, alternately circular and square, the latter each of sufficient size to contain a cabinet, or small room.

Hay's house at Park with the fifteen or more which Thomas MacLellan of Bombie was able to provide at his Kirkcudbright mansion.

A notable group of castles, either built from new or substantially remodelled at this date, survives in the Northern Isles. They share so many common architectural details that it comes as no surprise to discover that they belong to one aristocratic family and were very likely built by one man, Andrew Crawford, master of work to the Stewart Earls of Orkney until his death at the outset of the seventeenth century. The first earl, Robert, was no humble laird but an illegitimate son of James V and commendator (or titular abbot) of Holyrood in 1564 when his half-sister, Queen Mary, first interested him in Orkney. By the time he was created its earl in 1581, Robert had acquired the reputation as a cruel and despotic ruler and upon his death in 1593 was succeeded by a son if anything more tyrannous. All their building work, we are reliably informed, was carried out with slave labour culled from a downtrodden tenantry, but it is truly astonishing that these two unprincipled scoundrels should, in the comparatively short time they ruled the Northern Isles, have erected so graceful and refined a group of castles as ever was built outwith monarchy. The first Earl's Palace, Birsay, built about a courtyard around 1574, is now sadly ruined, though the west façade still gives an impression of austere grandeur. The castles built by the son, the Earl's Palace, Kirkwall and Scalloway, his seat on Shetland, both built at the very outset of the seventeenth century, together with Muness, erected in 1598 by an uncle of Earl Patrick and an equally unsavoury individual, one Laurence Bruce, are three remarkable structures. The Earl's Palace in Kirkwall, in particular, with its splendid hall and articulate use of bay and oriel windows, is the culmination of all that is good in castle planning and design and has rightly been hailed as "possibly the most mature and accomplished piece of Renaissance architecture left in Scotland".

Be it tower-house, palace-house or otherwise, each new property shared with its neighbour numerous features which clearly set them apart from castles of an earlier age. In particular, defensive considerations were noticeably exercising the minds of builders less and less as they contrived to improve on those aspects touching on comfort and domestic convenience. They were enabled to do this because the increased power and authority of central

Culross Palace, the residence of an enterprising businessman and industrialist with interests in commerce and coal, not a member of the landed gentry. But society was changing now, and power and riches were no longer the sole prerogative of those owning the land.

The Earl's Palace at Kirkwall, justly hailed as "possibly the most mature and accomplished piece of Renaissance architecture left in Scotland". The elaborately decorated projecting corner turrets on the left, part of Earl Patrick Stewart's bed-chamber, and the equally ornate oriel window and chimney-breast belonging to his great hall beyond (see illustration on page 10) are those "additional fantasies" grafted onto a highly sophisticated internal plan, which result in the very highest standard of castle construction at this late date, "all formed out of a builder's brain".

67

The "busy" wall-top at Claypotts, complete with ornate semi-circular headed dormer window, crow-stepped gable and corbelled angles.

A projecting, corbelled corner turret, or bartizan, at Newark Castle. Note the attention to symmetry with the "blind" window to the left of the real one.

and burn baillis according to the accoustomat ordour observit as sic tymes upoun the bordouris". Wall-tops now became the focus of attention of builders for a different, altogether more peaceable reason, as each exercised considerable architectural ingenuity in the manner in which wall related to roof. At Claypotts the wall-head is particularly well-contrived and pleasing to the eye. The round projecting towers are topped by square garrets ingeniously contrived through the use of continuous corbelling, whilst the tasteful incorporation of dormer windows, crow-stepped gables and prominent chimney stacks adds much to the charm. A favourite ploy was the use of mock machicolations in addition to continuous corbelling, further accentuating the interest and activity at the wall-top.

External elevations otherwise were generally uninteresting. The majority were harled, or roughcast, rendering them quite plain to the passer-by. It was usual for there to be a sculpted panel above the main doorway bearing the arms of the lord, and sometimes his lady, together with incidental information – a date perhaps or some wise maxim. A visitor to Maxwell's home at Drumcoltran was urged to "conceal what is secret; speak little; be truthful; avoid wine; remember death; be merciful", and we can scarce imagine this particular laird's house witnessing much "belly cheer".

Defensive considerations were not entirely forsaken. Though windows now became quite sizeable, and particularly generous within the principal rooms, iron grilles and bars were frequently applied to the outside to secure the house from intruders. They could also unintentionally prevent egress as the unfortunate incident at Elcho in 1630 illustrates. During a fire one night, several of Lord Wemyss' noble guests were burnt alive as they fought in vain to effect their escape through the heavily grated windows. At some castles, Claypotts and Tolquhon, for example, the distribution of gun-loops throughout has quite clearly been carefully considered, ensuring that all exterior wall-faces and openings were adequately covered from within. At others, like Greenknowe, they are so haphazardly sited and tactically inept it is as if the builder saw them merely as ornamentation. But there is no doubt as to the stern intention behind those incorporated into Burleigh and Elcho for there have survived some of the timber cills into which the spur or rowlock-shaped swivel support for the long barrel of the gun was set.

government had combined to make private castles redundant as military targets. Only when there was a breakdown in central administration, as during the revolution of the 1640s, did castles come again, though briefly, into the spotlight as centres of warfare.

The provision of battlements upon wall-tops, so vital to castle garrisons in former times, was scarcely considered now, although they look functional enough over the entrance tower at Elcho, at Drumcoltran and elsewhere. The two short stretches of defended wall-walk grafted onto the summit of Smailholm may indeed have been in earnest for an Act of Council, dated 1587, directed Scots lieges to "keip watch nyght and day,

An essay in Renaissance architectural detailing – the main façade of Patrick Maxwell's "new wark" at Newark Castle. The obsession with symmetry had been so all-pervading that the builder of the new residence of 1590 has changed the external appearance of the fifteenth-century tower-house on the far right (the quoins, or corner-stones, of this older residence are distinctly visible as a vertical line in the fabric).

left
The entrance-doorway into Newark Castle with its blithesome statement above.

right
A heavily grilled window at Elcho Castle.

69

A gun-hole at Elcho Castle with a hagbut of croc, a muzzle-loaded gun of the type then common throughout Scotland. The wrought-iron stem would have had a wooden stock. The gun (in the Royal Museum of Scotland's collection) has a spike near the mouth of the barrel which slots into a hole in the wooden cill, allowing the gun to be secured and traversed. The operation of loading and firing can have been none other than clumsy and tiresome.

A chamber in Newark Castle with much of its timber furnishings intact. On the right, a door into the privy, or toilet-closet; in the centre, wall panelling containing a cupboard; on the left, a wall-chamber that once contained a press-bed, or folding bed; overhead, brightly painted ceiling joists.

A wide-mouthed, horizontal gun-hole at Spynie Palace, typical of the new style that first appeared in Scotland early in the sixteenth-century as a successor to the old vertical loops (see illustration of Newark Castle on page 69).

Within the castle walls the emphasis continued to be laid upon an improvement in the domestic planning. The generally smaller households employed by these lesser lairds enabled their houses to become more fully self-contained. Where formerly there would have been an array of service offices and domestic accommodation spread about the main residence, now all was integrated into a single unit as far as was possible. In particular, the kitchen was now more handily situated, generally at ground level and with its ancillary offices and store-rooms close by. The floor above continued to house the more public apartments, but the provision of back-stairs for the use of domestic staff enabled the principal stair to become a more grand show-piece, such as we see at Newark, Crichton and elsewhere. The public rooms became increasingly light and airy, often with quite splendid fenestration and none more so perhaps than Earl Patrick Stewart's palace at Kirkwall, whose great hall was among the noblest state rooms of any lord's castle in Scotland. Private chambers ceased to be poky little closets carved out of the castle walls but now became plentiful, of a good size and fitted with the necessary amenities. At Lord Maxwell's castle at Newark, completed in 1599, one bed-chamber still retains much of its original fixtures and fittings – the painted ceiling, pine-panelled walls, fireplace, toilet-closet and, a rare survival indeed, the bed-recess, precisely like that described by Fynes Moryson, a visitor to Scotland in 1598: "their bedsteads were then like cubbards in the wall, with doores to be opened and shut at pleasure, so as we climbed up to our beds".

The significant advances in domestic planning achieved within the castle were mirrored by

The exquisite formal garden at Edzell Castle, viewed from the lord's hall in the tower-house. The summer house in the far corner served as a retreat from the main residence.

equally beneficial developments in the grounds and policies around. We know little of the horticultural inclinations of lords in earlier times. What is clear is that from the sixteenth century on, a greater attention was devoted to improvements in the environs of these noble residences. Gardens, in particular, became important adjuncts to the house, wherein exercise and relaxation could be pleasurably taken and intimacy more easily achieved. James Douglas, 4th Earl of Morton, Chancellor then Regent of Scotland from 1572, "busied himself in making walls and alleys, in drawing of garden plots" and the remnant of a once-stately garden at his castle at Aberdour can yet be detected. The so-called "King's Knot", a formal garden perhaps originally laid out for James I below the ramparts of Stirling, has survived a good deal better and retains something of its former grandeur. But by far the most instructive and pleasurable survival is Sir David Lindsay's remarkable pleasance at Edzell, completed in 1604. Here the formal parterre is enclosed by a garden wall of unusual richness, with bays containing recesses for flower boxes and holes for nesting birds, and elaborately carved panels depicting the planetary deities. At one corner is a summer-house, a delightful little building designed as a retreat from the main castle from which the garden could be enjoyed without having to brave the elements. The ground floor was a banqueting-room where sweetmeats could be enjoyed after the main repast. In another corner of the garden is a bath-house containing bath, dressing-room and sitting-room. Truly, castles were fast ceasing to look like prisons, as one traveller noted, and to have more the appearance of "houses of reception . . . with good walks and gardens about them".

Public Works and
Private Homes

CASTLES were the product of a feudal society. They were the visible expression of lordship, that is the control of the land and its indwellers. As the structure and government of the nation changed during the course of the Middle Ages, so lordly fortress-residences came to be anachronisms. Whilst castles dominated the land, they dominated warfare and the need for strong defences was crucial. But when the military importance of castles waned, so also did the requirement to fortify. Once-mighty fortress-residences became great country mansions, and the lofty towers of the lesser nobility gave way to fashionable lairds' houses.

The change was effected only gradually. Craignethan may have been the last of the truly medieval castles to be built, in the middle of the sixteenth century, but defensive considerations were still exercising the minds of the landowning class until well into the following century. Although it is clear that some devices of medieval fortification were now being incorporated merely as ornament into the façades of their residences, many yet retained fully functioning elements, principally gun-loops, no doubt on account of "the state of war and constant animosities between their families". The fear of many now was one of personal insecurity. "Please God," vowed one laird, "I will build me such a house as thieves will need to knock at ere they enter." On occasion, localised conditions of instability were exacerbated by disorders on a national scale, as during the revolution and Cromwellian interlude of the 1640s and 1650s. At this time, many castles became the focus, albeit briefly, of warfare on the grand scale and several of the larger fortresses were subjected to sieges such as they had never yet experienced. At Huntly and Hermitage, earthen gun-emplacements (called ravelins), specifically erected during the Civil War to protect the garrisons within, can still be seen as grass-covered triangular-shaped mounds. Again, in the troublous days following the Revolution of 1689, certain castles once more featured in the national debate and one, Kilchurn, beside Loch Awe in the west Highlands, was radically altered by John Campbell, 1st Earl of Breadalbane, in the 1690s to provide secure barrack accommodation for his private army.

The concept of mounted knights and other armed vassals fighting in the service of their lord was central to the feudal system, but as national government became stronger so the notion of a permanent standing army began to take root. Hitherto the national army, the Scottish host, had been raised only when the need arose and disbanded thereafter. The situation changed largely as a result of the occupation of Scotland by Protector Cromwell's "model army" between 1650 and 1660. Edinburgh Castle was first selected as his headquarters and from this time on the Great Hall of James IV ceased to play host to prestigious ceremonial occasions and became little more than a soldiers' barrack. It was a similar story at Stirling. Gone was the age of the private retainer fighting in the defence of his lord and castle; the time of the professional soldier, housed in garrisons built at the nation's expense, had come.

Though fragments of the forts built for the Protector at Ayr, Leith, and elsewhere have

opposite
Fort George, from above the Moray Firth, one of the most outstanding artillery fortifications in all Europe and little changed from the time of its completion in 1769.

73

The pentagonal-shaped Fort Charlotte, delineated in red on this aerial view, is now difficult to appreciate at street level where it is hemmed in on all sides by more recent buildings.

A Victorian photograph of some of the armament then mounted at Fort Charlotte and guarding the Sound of Bressay.

buildings within for, though the fort has survived remarkably well, much of the present complex dates from the 1780s when the place was repaired and rearmed by the Hanoverian government following the escapades of the renegade Paul Jones around the coast of his native land in 1778–79.

The gravest threat by far to the stability of the country came with the landing of William, Prince of Orange, at Torbay in 1688. The likelihood of a protracted struggle between the Williamites and the Jacobites became apparent from the outset, as evinced by the speed with which the pro-government Campbell Earl of Breadalbane set about the re-shaping of his castle at Kilchurn the year after. The government itself was not long in following suit. During the reign of Queen Anne, which witnessed in 1707 the joining together in a parliamentary Union of the two "auld enemies", Scotland and England, a large barrack for officers was erected on the citadel at Edinburgh Castle (now the home of the Scottish United Services Museum) and ambitious schemes for vast outer defences instigated both here and at Stirling. The work at Edinburgh did not progress very far, but the approach to Stirling is today dominated by Queen Anne's outer defence, designed by the engineer Theodore Dury. The death of Anne in 1714 and the succession of George I, Elector of

survived, none is in state care. Shortly after the "restoration" of Charles II in 1660, however, England went to war with Holland and, as part of the king's defensive strategy, an artillery fortification was begun in 1665 at Lerwick to protect the Sound of Bressay. Fort Charlotte took the form of a pentagonal-shaped bastioned fort, typical of the period, with a massive seaward-facing wall punctuated by gun embrasures. Little can be written as to the nature of the garrison

Hanover, rather than James VIII and III, the Old Pretender, sparked off the rebellion of a year later, the '15, as it has come to be known, and although the rising was successfuly suppressed the confidence of the Hanoverian government was so shaken that severe measures were taken in an attempt to snuff out all remaining Jacobite sympathisers.

Foremost among these was a renewed building programme, including the erection of four new infantry garrisons in the Highlands whence regular troops could maintain law and order. The barracks at Ruthven, built between 1719 and 1721 on the site of the Comyn castle in Badenoch, stands today practically complete save for the roofs over the two piles of barracks, intended to house up to 120 men, with their officers separately accommodated. In 1734, following a recommendation by Major-General Wade, a stable was added for the use of up to twenty-eight dragoons stationed there and acting as convoys on the important network of roads then being constructed in this part of the Highlands.

Major-General Wade had, six years earlier, been asked to advise on all fortifications in Scotland. Edinburgh Castle he conceived to be "a place of the greatest importance to the safety of that part of your Majesty's Dominions" and consequently a further building programme was put in hand. Much of Edinburgh's defensive circuit, particularly along the north and west flanks, was built to the designs of Captain John Romer, military engineer under Wade. The Governor's House (built 1742), a "pleasingly restrained classical building", was the principal garrison building erected at this time. Romer was engaged also on designs for the refortification of the royal castle at Dumbarton in the west of the country. Here too the artillery defences are particularly well preserved, as is the Governor's House, erected in 1735.

Whilst work proceeded apace at Dumbarton and Edinburgh at the nation's expense, William Duff, a wealthy landowner later to become Baron Braco and Earl of Fife, was digging deep into his own purse to erect a splendid private mansion on his estate close to Banff. In some respects Duff House, and other great country houses of like manner, have much in common with the mighty fortress-residences of the medieval age. Just as Walter of Moray desired to display his wealth and manifest his social standing by creating a powerful stone castle on his lands at Bothwell, so too was Duff persuaded to do likewise. But whereas the former

One of two piles of barracks at Ruthven, built between 1719 and 1721. Each barrack was designed to accommodate sixty enlisted men, each of the six rooms containing "five beds for ten men in as little room as can be well allowed".

Officers were quartered in small pavilions adjacent. The well at bottom left was the only element from the late medieval castle of the Gordon Earls of Huntly retained and used by the Hanoverian garrison.

The Governor's House and King George's Battery at Dumbarton Castle, built in the 1730s to designs by Captain John Romer, military engineer for Scotland.

Duff House, intended as the grandiose residence of William Duff, Lord Braco, an ambitious man who desired not only to succeed but to be seen by all as so doing. His mansion, designed by William Adam in 1735, was intended as an undeniable statement of his wealth and standing. It has been described as "a medieval castle in Baroque dress", though it is pure residence, not in the least fortress.

Corgarff Castle, in remote Strathdon, a sixteenth-century tower-house converted in 1748 to a soldiers' barrack and greatly strengthened by the addition of a star-shaped musketry wall. Note the remnant of a projecting stone machicolation over the one doorway into the tower, a survival from its time as a medieval tower and of no use to the Redcoats.

was a feudal baron the latter was a Whig politician. Gone from Duff House are all the artifices of war. Nonetheless, the result of his endeavours has, with justification, been described as "a medieval castle in Baroque dress". Bothwell Castle and Duff House have one more thing in common. Neither was completed to the original designs. We can only assume that the work on Bothwell was interrupted by war; Duff House remained unfinished as a result of a breakdown in relations between the client and his architect, William Adam.

Whilst the law-suit over the building of Duff House dragged on through the courts, William Adam became contracted to the Hanoverian government to assist in the reconstruction of the Cromwellian fort at Inverness. The designer was William Skinner, newly appointed as military engineer for North Britain, the year 1746. The most threatening Jacobite rising had only recently been bloodily crushed by William Augustus, Duke of Cumberland, the king's brother. Before work began, a halt had to be called and a new site hastily commandeered as the base for George II's army. Upon the "barren, sandy point" projecting into the Moray Firth 20 km north-east of Inverness chosen by Skinner was built one of the outstanding artillery fortifications in all of Europe, Fort George, described in 1748 by Lt.-Col. James Wolfe as "the most considerable fortress and best situated in Great Britain". It stands today in almost the same condition as it was left upon completion of the contract in 1769. What is so very special about Fort George is that not only does the entire multi-bastioned defence with its outworks survive entire, but that all the garrison buildings – officers' blocks, barrack piles, ordnance and provision stores, guardhouses, powder stores, even the chapel – remain within its ramparts also. William Adam died shortly before construction work began in 1748, but his three sons, John, Robert and James, retained the masonry contract and saw the great work completed. William Skinner, the fort's creator, was honoured by a grateful monarch with the first governorship of the garrison. Under his control and residing also in the fort were two infantry battalions (1600 officers and men) with an artillery unit to man the defences. The cost to the public purse amounted in the end to well over £200,000, equivalent to the gross national product of Scotland at the time, and not so much as one cartridge was shot from its ramparts in anger. Fort George, it has been said, was so powerful, like Edward I of England's castle at Caerphilly in Wales, that it had no history.

Whilst work began on Fort George, two smaller barracks were created out of existing tower-houses. That at Corgarff Castle, formerly the property of one of the Forbes name, had featured in the revolution of the 1640s and in all the Jacobite risings. It now became a centre from which the Hanoverian army could police the wilds of Strathdon and maintain law and order. The Battle of Culloden, however, proved to be the last battle fought on Scottish, indeed British, soil. No further warfare was threatened from within her boundaries and thereafter all defences erected were associated solely with threats from across the seas. Fort Charlotte and other coastal forts were repaired and re-equipped as a result of the wars with America and France towards the end of the eighteenth century and further threats of invasion occasioned the construction of, amongst others, the Martello tower at Hackness, on Scapa Flow in Orkney, in 1813, the coastal battery on the seaward flank of Fort George in 1860 and the anti-aircraft batteries upon Dumbarton Castle rock during the Second World War.

A barrack-room within the erstwhile Great Hall at Stirling Castle (see illustration on page 60). The arched head of one of two windows flanking the dais can just be made out.

above left
An Armstrong 64-pounder rifled gun (1865) mounted on a bastion at Fort George.

Hackness Martello Tower, built in 1813 as part of the coastal defence works guarding Scapa Flow during the troubled time of the Napoleonic Wars.

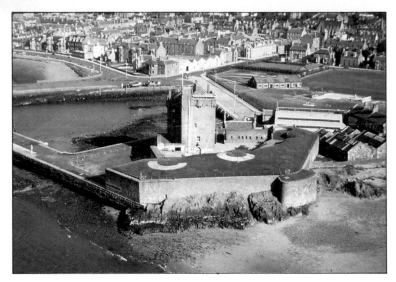

left
Broughty Castle, beside the Tay estuary, a fifteenth-century tower-house converted to a coastal defence battery in 1860–61.

below
Dumbarton Castle, from a late seventeenth-century engraving. There is no other place in Scotland that has a longer recorded history as a place of strength and it was rightly seen in the Middle Ages as "a castell stronge and harde for to obteine".

There is perhaps no more fitting place for this story to end than atop this volcanic plug of basalt dominating the estuary of the Clyde, for there is no other place in Scotland that has a longer recorded history as a place of strength. Nothing now survives of the ancient capital of the Britons of Strathclyde, and very little, sadly, of the medieval royal castle. Much of what remains above ground is of the seventeenth and eighteenth centuries. This craggy, impregnable stronghold somehow speaks for all those castles, towers and fortress-residences which Scotsmen, and others, erected throughout the country in the medieval period, for Dumbarton, like them, was "a castell stronge and harde for to obteine".